Great Cities of Eastern Europe

Roger Rapoport

John Muir Publications
Santa Fe, New Mexico

For my father

John Muir Publications, P.O. Box 613, Santa Fe, NM 87504

First edition. First printing December 1991

Library of Congress Cataloging-in-Publication Data

Rapoport, Roger.
  Great cities of Eastern Europe / Roger Rapoport. — 1st ed.
    p. cm.
  Includes index.
  ISBN 1-56261-012-0
  1. Europe, Eastern—Description and travel—1981-   2. Cities and
towns—Europe, Eastern.   I. Title.
DJK19.R37   1992
914.7'.04—dc20   91-30292
                                                 CIP

Distributed to the book trade by
W.W. Norton & Co., Inc.
New York, New York

Design: Sally Blakemore
Cover art: Tony D'Agostino
Maps: Don Curry
Typography: Copygraphics, Inc.
Printer: McNaughton & Gunn

Great Cities
of Eastern Europe

CONTENTS

ACKNOWLEDGMENTS

Six writers and researchers made invaluable contributions to this book. Christine Schoefer worked on the Germany section and also contributed to the introduction. In Poland, Ewa Malicka Kingston, a native of that country, did excellent research and writing. Daniela Mankova, who works in the Prague travel industry, provided extensive assistance in her country. In Hungary, Rita Szekeres and Katalin Koronczi both provided excellent research assistance. Finally, Linda Moyer, the co-author of *Undiscovered Islands of the Mediterranean* (Santa Fe, N.M.; John Muir Publications, 1990) and *Undiscovered Islands of the U.S. and Canadian West Coast* (Santa Fe, N.M.: John Muir Publications, 1992), worked on the Yugoslavia section.

I would also like to acknowledge the assistance of Peter Beren, Robert and Nancy Maynard, Roy Aarons, Belinda Taylor, Bari Brenner, Burl Willes, Ellen Thatcher, Charles Kingston, Terry Doran, Tom Duncan, my wife, Margot, and children, Jonathan and Elizabeth, the Jirsak family in Prague, the tourist offices of Germany, Berlin, Hungary, Czechoslovakia, Poland, and Yugoslavia, and, once again, the staff of John Muir Publications.

PREFACE

E very guidebook begins with a disclaimer. Here's mine: The author of this book takes no responsibility for any reader falling in love with Eastern Europe and never wanting to come home. This year more than six million Americans will travel to Europe. Unfortunately, most of them will never see the "Real Europe" that is the focus of this book. If you have been to eastern Germany, Poland, Czechoslovakia, Hungary, or Yugoslavia, you know what makes this region special. If you haven't, we urge you to visit soon to enjoy the special Old World charm of a destination that is blessedly behind the times.

Even before the fall of the Berlin Wall and the liberation of these Eastern European nations, there were many good reasons to go. Czechoslovakia has more castles than France, and many of them compare favorably with the best in Europe. Eastern Germany has some of the most fascinating big and little cities found anywhere as well as lovely countryside where it is still possible to ride on scheduled steam trains. Poland, one of the most underrated nations in Europe, is a gem, with cities, like Krakow, that are World Heritage sites. And when you explore Budapest's restaurants or Sopron's historic district, you'll know why Hungary is such a favorite with knowledgeable Europeans.

Only now, several years after the fall of the wall, is this message beginning to reach American travelers. Caught up in the political excitement that has gripped this region, many came home with glowing reports of the people, the food, the antiquities, and, of course, the prices that are a fraction of those in Western Europe. But until now no guidebook has been available to gently show you the way to the very best of this vast region.

What makes Eastern Europe unique is the Communist era that began in 1945. Even the casual visitor can find traces of this life if he or she knows what to look for. You will notice the distinctive architecture and city planning, study public statues and murals, and read about the trials of former Communist officials accused of looting the state.

Eastern Europe is a world in transition where even the street names are changing day by day. For the traveler with the latest map in hand, this region offers a rare opportunity to glimpse history struggling with the future, the collision of command and market economies, and, of course, East confronting West. As the old society disintegrates, this region offers the political sightseeing opportunity of a lifetime to the traveler who wants more than grand photo opportunities and Socialist souvenirs.

As you travel through Eastern Europe, you'll learn there was much more to it than state control, surveillance, intimidation, and the wall. Despite the oppression of the Communists, these nations were not a Gulag. Women had great freedom of movement because the streets were not a dangerous place. Cities were not ghettoized, screenwriters and artists lived in the same buildings as shift workers and engineers; the bureaucracy, not money or status, decided who got an apartment where. Such things were the result of socialism. But many of the region's most notable features came from the absence of capitalism—the warped sense of time, the intensity of friendships, the absence of constant sensory assaults through advertisements.

There was a saying in East Germany that applied to the entire region: "In the West, everything goes and nothing matters, while in the East, nothing goes and everything matters."

Out of necessity, people in the East were used to having a great deal of contact with each other. Everyone cultivated the favor of sales clerks and car mechanics because they might be needed at some future time. They informed neighbors of the availability of bananas or cotton socks in the stores and set up complex informal trade networks. The absence of a glitzy entertainment scene also encouraged people to focus on each other. Furthermore, in a general atmosphere of distrust and suspicion, friendships deepened. In the East, people visited each other without scheduling times in advance. Instead of using answering machines, people left messages on small notepads tacked to doors.

Westernization is making these networks obsolete. The market economy substitutes money for goods and anonymity for connections. The fast pace of life will discourage the small-town familiarity that many Eastern Europeans took for granted. The blaring of the Western media has begun to drown out the oral culture. Many people of the East, who found it easy to live rather unconventionally beyond the reach of state politics on a minimal income, will miss the niches they created for themselves. They relied on the network of social services, subsidized rents, dirt cheap bread and milk, and occasional packages sent by relatives and friends from the West. Predictably, all these things, including the packages, are disappearing. Today they face a dire choice: join the rat race or be poor.

This sense—that things that would scarcely merit a nod or a raised eyebrow in Berkeley or West Berlin suddenly had weight— still lingers today. But the pace of life has quickened, people's priorities and necessities, their questions and answers, have shifted dramatically. Today Eastern Europeans embrace the Western future eagerly, breathlessly tossing out the old regime's symbols and insignia, Westernizing—to the extent that they can afford it—their wardrobes and their homes. Instead of monotonous store shelves, you will see the dawn of the used car lot; instead of long lines at the supermarkets, you are likely to discover queues at unemployment offices. Neon advertising signs and banners are beginning to replace red and white Socialist motivational banners.

This is the unique and unforgettable story you will see with the help of *Great Cities of Eastern Europe*. Research for this first edition began several weeks after the fall of the wall. Along with a team of six other veteran writers and researchers, I crisscrossed Eastern Europe. Collectively, we visited every establishment and sight recommended in this book. We checked our choices against the judgments of local experts and, finally, settled on the "great cities." We believe you'll find this trip the journey of a lifetime.

It is no secret that back before the 1989 revolution, when the state controlled the tourism industry and overcharged tourists, traveling in this region had its complexities and limitations. But I am delighted to report that today travel here has never been easier and, I would like to add, more fairly priced. Visas are not required in any of these countries. Private pensions are now available for the first time in towns and villages across the region. No matter what price range you choose, from a $10-a-night room in a private apartment in Budapest to a $75- to $100-a-night apartment on Prague's Old Town Square, we guarantee you will find excellent values. This book tells you how to find the best restaurants where you won't have to wait in line, how to find vegetarian food, how to travel efficiently, where to find the best shopping, and most of all, how to meet the fascinating people who make traveling through this region such a pleasure.

Traveling in all four seasons, we learned how to take advantage of this area at any time of year and, best of all, how to enjoy a trip that's trouble-free, moderately priced, and memorable. A note of warning. As you research your trip, you will doubtless find many references to the prerevolutionary period. Keep in mind that any travel literature written prior to 1990 is outdated. Street names have changed (more than 150 in Budapest alone, reflecting the demise of Communist names), new hotels and restaurants have sprung up, visa and currency requirements have been dropped, unleaded gas supplies are increasing, and so on. The proliferation of hundreds of private tour companies and booking services has completely transformed this area and given you many delightful new options and better prices. Clearly, the tourist is one of the early beneficiaries of these new governments.

As you look through these pages, you may notice that some places recommended in other guides do not appear here. In fact, entire countries, such as Romania, are not included in this book. Although we have great admiration for the Romanian people and their effort to reclaim their nation from the Communists, we do not believe it is a good vacation destination at this time. Other guidebook authors will tell you how they, as Westerners carrying special gas coupons, were allowed to cut around six-hour lines at gas stations. This does not square with our image of responsible tourism. In addition, there seems something wrong about touting the cuisine of a nation where the people do not have enough to eat. We hope that liberation will quickly improve life for the Romanian people and that this country can be included in the next edition. Positive steps, such as closing down some of the country's most polluting industries, have already begun.

Finally, John Muir Publications' commitment to timely travel information means you can rest assured this book is not a retread of past trips but an up-to-date, original work that reflects contemporary Eastern Europe. And now, come with us to lift up the time capsule and see this unforgettable region at a watershed moment in its complex and fascinating history.

The East: Seeing the Real Europe

Planning a trip to Eastern Europe has never been easier thanks to the political changes of the past several years. Many of the limitations and restrictions of years past have been eliminated. The relatively modest expense of touring in these countries—everything except gas is cheaper than in the United States or Western Europe —will easily compensate for the cost of your plane flight. In fact, if you are planning an extended trip, a visit to Eastern Europe will compare favorably with any vacation you have in mind. And even if you are planning a short stay, you will find that your days in Eastern Europe will easily offset the price of traveling in Western Europe.

Because this region is compact and very accessible, you do not need a great deal of time to enjoy a visit here. Although two weeks or longer are recommended, a ten-day visit can be an excellent way to sample the region. Visiting all the cities recommended in our book would take at least a month, probably five weeks. I recommend allowing a minimum of one week to visit the destinations we cover in Eastern Germany, Poland, Czechoslovakia, or Hungary. Plan at least three days for Dubrovnik, longer if you want to enjoy some of the nearby islands and other historic cities.

GETTING THERE

No visas are required for a visit to any of these cities. You can begin your trip in any of the major cities such as Berlin, Prague, Budapest, or Warsaw. But you may find the airfares are better to either Frankfurt or Vienna, both excellent gateways for this trip. Many airlines such as Lufthansa, United, TWA, American, Delta, Northwest, SAS, Air France, Malev, and CSA provide scheduled service to Eastern Europe or to Frankfurt and Vienna, where you can make easy connections to this region. In addition to scheduled service, your travel agent may be able to arrange a less expensive charter flight or buy you a ticket from a consolidator, a wholesaler who discounts the price of the scheduled ticket and advertises heavily in Sunday travel sections of papers like the *Los Angeles Times, New York Times, Chicago Tribune,* and *Village Voice.* When making arrangements through a consolidator, your seat is typically on a scheduled carrier, but you pay less than if you buy direct from the airline. Because trip cancellation penalties frequently apply, you will want to buy enough trip cancellation insurance to cover you in the event of unforeseen circumstances. It typically costs $5.50 per $100. Only buy enough coverage to pay the penalty that would be assessed if you change your mind. One of the best programs we know about is offered by Travel Guard at 800/826-1300 (in Wisconsin, 800/634-0644).

GETTING AROUND

Rail travel is a convenient way to visit this region. You need to buy a Eurailpass before leaving the United States. Offered in a variety of combinations, it is valid in two of the countries discussed in this book, Germany and Hungary. If you plan to do a lot of train travel there as well as in the fifteen other Western European countries covered by the program, consider buying a Eurailpass. You can get fifteen consecutive days of unlimited first-class train travel for $390 or buy a flexipass that gives you five days of travel within any fifteen-day period for $230. In addition, a youth pass for travelers under 26 is valid for fifteen days of travel within a three-month period. The German railroad has a pass good for travel within that country. Even though your Eurailpass will not be valid in Czechoslovakia, Poland, and Yugoslavia, you may still find the train is the most economical way to travel in this region. Remember, before boarding a train in Yugoslavia, you'll want to check the latest traveler's advisories from the State Department as explained in the Yugoslavia section of this book.

DRIVING

Because some of the best sightseeing in Eastern Europe is in the backcountry, consider renting a car for at least part of your trip. Your best bet is to call one of the major American companies that affiliate with European companies or have branches overseas. Since some of these companies have restrictions on insurance coverage in Eastern Europe or, in the case of Avis, will not rent cars to go into Poland because of theft problems, your choices may be limited. Rental prices are higher in most of the Eastern European countries than in the West. As a result, you are usually better off renting your car in either Germany or Austria and then returning it to the same country. You must make your reservation before you leave the United States if you want to get the best deal.

We paid our own way to research this book and accepted no sponsorship of any kind. Our opinion is that at the current time Hertz offers the best car rental deal. For around $220 a week, you can rent a subcompact car in Germany or Austria with unlimited mileage and full insurance coverage. The car can be driven anywhere on our itinerary, and there is no drop charge as long as you return it to a station within the renting country. Ironically, because some of the autobahns in Eastern Germany are torn up for reconstruction, you may find that it is easier to drive through this region on secondary roads. Another possibility would be to use trains in Germany and then rent your car near the border, say, in Berlin, if you are headed for Poland, or in Dresden, if you are on your way to Czechoslovakia. Remember, if you plan to drive in eastern Germany, allow plenty of extra time on the autobahn as delays are significant and driving two-lane roads is beautiful but slow. While you may not have much use for your car in cities where mass transit is excellent, you'll find it extremely convenient to drive to regions like Czechoslovakia's South Bohemia or Hungary's Sopron/Kőszeg area. If you are traveling with several people, a car may also be your best transportation deal.

If you are driving, we ask that you follow a few simple precautions to guarantee a smooth trip. First, never leave anything valuable in your vehicle. It is always a good idea to park it in an attended garage when you are in a city. Night driving is discouraged, especially in rural areas where visibility and signage can be poor and deer frequently cross the road. Never drive with less than half a tank of gas. Gas stations are limited in rural areas, and unleaded gasoline is in short supply in Hungary, Czechoslovakia, and Poland. For your convenience, we have named the locations of unleaded gas stations on your route in this book. In Germany, you can also stop by the office of the ADAC auto club in any city and pick up a copy of their map that gives the location of all unleaded gas stations throughout Europe. Remember, in Czechoslovakia, only coupons purchased at banks, major hotels, and Čedok offices can be used by foreigners to buy gas. Be sure to bring hard currency (traveler's checks are also accepted at some locations) to pay for these coupons. Make sure you get coupons that specify unleaded.

Finally, because of political difficulties in parts of Yugoslavia, we do not recommend driving to Dubrovnik. If you are touring by car, we suggest you see the northern countries first and then fly or take a ship to Yugoslavia. The Yugoslav coast can be reached from several Italian cities by ferry.

MONEY

Because you may arrive late at night or on a holiday when banks are closed, bring along enough local currency to last you for one day in each country. Several hundred dollars worth of hard currency, useful in all kinds of situations, is highly recommended—either U.S. dollars or German marks. Because the banks in Eastern Europe will not sell you hard currency, you must bring it with you or purchase it in Western Europe. Also bring along a well-known brand of traveler's checks, but do not expect them to be accepted at every local shop or restaurant. Credit cards are useful, especially in major cities. Always carry your money in a money belt.

TELEPHONE

Do not expect telephone service in Eastern Europe to be like that in the West. Especially in eastern Germany, circuits are jammed and calls during the day can be hard to make. In general, it is best to make calls early or late in the day or on weekends. To telephone home, use USA Direct. You dial a local access code that connects you with an American operator. Your call is billed at the operator-assisted rate to your home telephone number. This is often much less expensive, and far less complicated, than going through the local telephone system. You can dial the access code yourself. If you have trouble getting through, your best bet is to stop by a local hotel and pay a small charge to have an operator or desk clerk dial the access code for you. Here are codes you'll need in countries where the service is available:

Germany: 01300-0010
Czechoslovakia 00-420-00101
Hungary: 171-499

HEALTH AND SAFETY

These are all safe countries to visit provided you take a few simple precautions. Keep your passport, cash, traveler's checks, and airline ticket in a money belt. Keep copies of your passport and plane ticket in a secure location. In general, purses are a magnet for trouble anywhere you travel. A better idea is to wear a backpack or fanny pack. Not only does it have more room for everything you need while walking around, it's very difficult to snatch. Do not even think about changing money on the black market. The slightly higher rate is not worth the potential difficulties. These are the people you want to avoid.

If you are concerned about the possibility of being treated in a foreign hospital, why not buy a medical evacuation policy from a company like Travel Assistance International (800/368-7878)? A $50 policy for two weeks gives you 24-hour coverage in the event of illness. If you need treatment, you will immediately be transported at their expense to a hospital with English-speaking staff in Western Europe. Or, if necessary, you will be flown home for care. By the way, do not forget to bring all your prescriptions with you.

RECOMMENDED READING

Although the fall of the wall invalidated the pre-1990 guidebook literature to this region, many fine books are available. Here are some of our favorites. All make great reading before, during, and after your trip.

Germany: If you can read only one book about Berlin, choose Christopher Isherwood's *Berlin Stories* (New York: New Directions). Its poignant description of how the Nazis came to power in the midst of the Weimar Republic era became the basis for the movie, *Cabaret*. Joel Agee's *Twelve Years* (New York: Farrar, Straus & Giroux) offers autobiographical reminiscences about an East German boyhood. Robert Darnton's *Berlin Journal, 1989-1990* (New York: W.W. Norton & Co.), is an eyewitness account of post-wall Berlin. Alfred Doblin's *Berlin, Alexanderplatz* (New York: Ungar Press) is a classic novel about the underside of Berlin in the 1920s. Although the wall is gone, John Le Carre's *The Spy Who Came in from the Cold* (New York: Bantam Books) never goes out of style. This classic spy thriller recaptures the tension of Cold War Berlin. Peter Schneider's *The Wall Jumper* (New York: Pantheon) offers short stories about life and love in divided Berlin. Kurt Vonnegut's *Slaughterhouse Five* (New York: Dell) is a classic account of the World War II bombing of Dresden. Finally, *Patterns of Childhood* (New York: Farrar, Straus & Giroux), by famed East German writer Christa Wolf, provides an autobiographical account of growing up in Hitler's Germany and life in the GDR.

Czechoslovakia: The *Insight Cityguide to Prague* (New York: Prentice Hall) is a good introduction to that city. You may also find the *Olympia Guide to Czechoslovakia* (Prague: Olympia) useful. Franz Kafka's *The Castle* (New York: Schocken) was banned by the Communists, the ultimate tribute to this writer. He will put you in the mood to visit Prague's famous Hradčany Castle. Milan Kundera's *The Unbearable Lightness of Being* (New York: Harper Collins) was made into a popular film. Václav Havel is an essayist as well as a playwright. Among his books is *Disturbing the Peace* (New York: Knopf).

Poland: The best guide to this country is Philip Ward's *Polish Cities* (Gretna, La.: Pelican). Jerzy Kosinski's *The Painted Bird* (New York: Modern Library) tells the story of a child walking about Eastern Europe during the Second World War. Nobel Prize-winning poet Czeslaw Milosz's *The Captive Mind* (New York: Random House) is also recommended.

Hungary: Andras Torok's *Budapest: A Critical Guide* (Budapest: Park) is an excellent guide to the capital. *Hungary: A Complete Guide*

(Budapest: Corvina) is also helpful. In addition, I recommend *Budapest 1900* (New York: Weidenfeld and Nicholson) for cultural background.

Yugoslavia: Rebecca West's *Black Lamb, Grey Falcon* (New York: Viking Press) is a good novel to read before leaving home. Also recommended are *Essentially Yugoslavia* by Celia Irving (London: Christopher Helm) and J. A. Cuddon's *The Companion Guide to Yugoslavia* (New York: Prentice Hall).

For political background on Eastern Europe, you may enjoy reading Timothy Garton Ash's *The Uses of Adversity* (New York: Vintage) as well as *The Magic Lantern* (New York: Random House). My book, *Into the Sunlight: Life After the Iron Curtain* (Berkeley: Heyday Books), offers a detailed look at the courageous men and women who ended the Communist era in Eastern Europe.

An excellent general guide, highly recommended for this trip, is Rick Steves's *Europe Through the Back Door* (Santa Fe: John Muir Publications). If you are planning additional travel in Western Europe, you'll find Rick's 2 to 22 Days Itinerary Planners covering countries like Germany, Austria, Switzerland, France, Great Britain, and Spain and Portugal invaluable.

Finally, every traveler to the countries covered in this volume needs to carry a phrase book in German, the Esperanto of the Eastern Bloc.

TOURIST OFFICES

These tourist offices can provide helpful background before you go:

Germany: German National Tourist Office, Suite 2230, 444 South Flower Street, Los Angeles, CA 90071. Tel. (213) 688-7332; Fax (213) 688-7574.

Czechoslovakia: Cedok, Suite 1902, 10 East 40th Street, New York, NY 10016. Tel. (212) 689-9720; Fax (212) 481-0597.

Hungary: Ibusz, One Parker Plaza, Suite 1104, Fort Lee, NJ 07024. Tel. (201) 592-8585; Fax (201) 592-8736.

Poland: Poland National Tourist Office, 333 N. Michigan Avenue, Chicago, IL 60601. Tel. (312) 236-9013.

Yugoslavia: Yugoslav National Tourist Office, Suite 20, 630 Fifth Avenue, New York, NY 10020. Tel. (212) 757-2801.

HELPFUL HINT

Whoever said the more things change, the more they remain the same must have been an armchair tourist. We urge you to confirm museum times, as well as plane and train reservations, in advance. Be sure to double check routes and expect street name changes and significant price fluctuations. It is a good idea to inquire locally before setting out for a destination. Always carry a good map, ideally purchased before you leave home. Bon voyage.

Eastern Germany

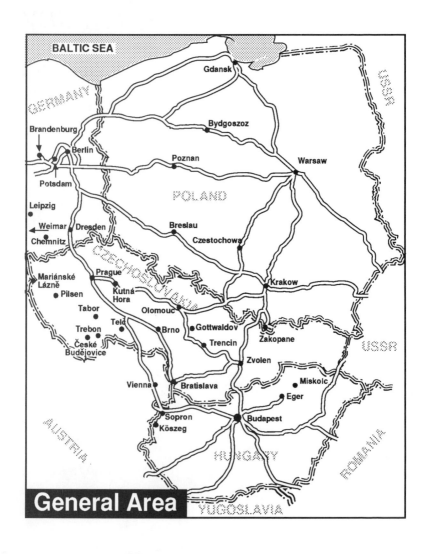

BALTIC SEA

General Area

Since 1945, access to the eastern half of Germany has been restricted to travelers by a plethora of visa requirements and transit regulations. The infamous Berlin Wall, built in 1961, was only the most visible symbol of East German inaccessibility. When the wall fell in November 1989, the doors opened wide to a new mecca for travelers: the five states of eastern Germany.

The newly unified Germany is a major political and economic player in the present world order. A modern, industrialized society, it has become a bridge between Eastern and Western Europe. Situated in the center of Europe, Germany prides itself on being future oriented. For the traveler, Germany is an ideal destination for other reasons: natural beauty, historical finds, and cultural delights. The wall created a kind of time capsule that preserved much of this region's impressive past. As you travel there, think of yourself strolling on a ridge (the present) from which you can glimpse the valley of the past (the Socialist GDR) to one side and the future (western Germany) on the other.

If you are traveling to Germany for the first time, you might be surprised how similar western Germany is to the United States. East Germany, which comprises about one-third of the land area of the German Federal Republic and one-third of the population (17 mil-

Berlin Wall near the Brandenburg Gate, Berlin

lion), has been virtually free of American influence. You may not even notice crossing from West to East—most traces of the wall have disappeared completely. But when you journey through the East, you will quickly appreciate the confrontation between the past and present, between the rich promise of the West and those who, for the first time in their lives, are unemployed. Although East German society, economy, and culture are being absorbed with breathtaking speed into the Western Federal Republic of Germany, they remain unique in many ways.

Germany's long history of provincialism is one explanation for the strong differences between East and West, which have survived the centralizing impulses of Hitler's regime as well as the division imposed by the Allied Powers after World War II. If you travel through the entire country, you will find regional identities much in evidence. You can watch geography and culture change from the reed-thatched roofs of lake-dotted Mecklenburg to industrialized Saxony where the infamous paper car, Trabant, was produced before the new owner, VW, took over; from the Harz mountains—home to spirits and witches who come, according to legend, to dance on the Blocksberg on Walpurgisnacht—to the fortified castles of Thuringia. The Saxony dialect is totally different from Berlin's. And, fortunately for the traveling gourmet, the cuisine—or *Küche*—also

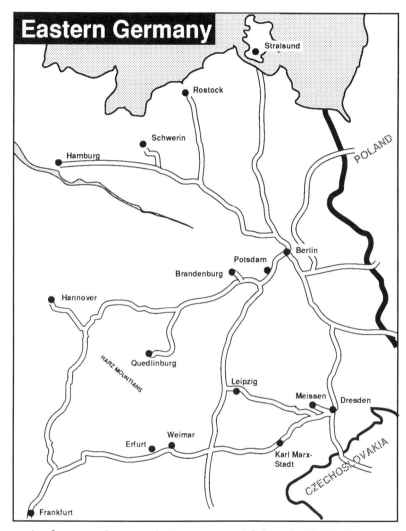

varies from north to south. I recommend fish in the Baltic Sea town of Warnemünde and Thüringer Klösse, a kind of potato dumpling, in Halle.

But the historic regional variations in dialect, culture, cuisine, customs, and even mentality are not the only explanation for eastern Germany's different flavor. A more crucial factor is the historical interlude of Communist rule and the absence of capitalism. This Germany was the site of a Socialist experiment that left its imprint despite its ultimate failure.

The East is a gold mine of German history. But which history? There is the "Old Germany": the ruins of the Holy Roman Empire within the German nation are more than a thousand years old. The castles, fortifications, and cathedrals are reminders of medieval fiefdoms and principalities. Splendid burgherhouses conjure up the era of prosperous mercantilism. The palaces and the grand boulevards bring to mind the German Empire. The Weimar Republic—Germany's twenties—is preserved in architecture and culture. And the ruins and the relics of Hitler's Third Reich continue to cast their shadows. Most of the countless sites of old German history are well preserved though few have been restored to their original beauty. All cast a historic spell enhanced by the fact that they escaped mass tourism, hawkers, vendors, and billboards for more than four decades.

Among the many rich possibilities in eastern Germany is the seventeeth-century harbor town of Stralsund on the Baltic Sea. Because virtually nothing in this town has been modernized, its mood invites romantic fantasies of schooners, clipper ships, and pirates. Or you can tour the Harz mountains, following the footsteps of Heinrich Heine who left a poetic travelog of his tour in the early nineteeth century. In the town of Quedlinburg, you will find the oldest half-timbered house in Germany, built around 1400. Quedlinburg's streets are too narrow for cars, ensuring that nothing will interfere with your quiet contemplation of the past.

Southern Thuringia, with its gently rolling hills, is the home of the Wartburg, probably Germany's most renowned castle. Built before the twelfth century, it harbors various historical eras within its fortified walls. Minstrels who sang here in the Middle Ages inspired Richard Wagner's opera "Tannhäuser." Martin Luther hid from his Catholic persecutors in the Wartburg and translated the New Testament in one of its spartan rooms. The city of Erfurt, in central Thuringia, dates back to the ninth century and flourished as one of Germany's most important medieval trade centers. Erfurt emanates an aura of faded wealth. Its most splendid buildings are situated around the large cobblestone marketplace surrounding the imposing Gothic cathedral and the Severi Church. Streets and lanes bear mercantile names, and the "Krämer" bridge is a small northern version of Florence's Ponte Vecchio.

Schloss Pfaueninsel, Berlin (Courtesy InterMarketing Berlin)

Saxony is probably East Germany's most famous province, and Leipzig, its capital, has recently gained notoriety as the heart of the popular protest movement that toppled the Communist government. This traditional trade fair city was known as the GDR's "keyhole to the world," because the large international trade fairs held during the Communist era brought a flood of foreign visitors. Thanks to them, Leipzig is relatively well equipped with cafés, teahouses, restaurants, and bars. It is the home of one of Germany's oldest universities, where the legendary Goethe studied, and is still the only East German city aside from Berlin with a cosmopolitan ambience.

Everywhere in eastern Germany, you will encounter reminders of national socialism and World War II, the result of an interesting combination of omission and conscious policy. The Communist government, short on funds for redevelopment, could easily resist the temptation so evident in the West to pave over most traces of Germany's tragic past in the postwar construction boom. Large cities have buildings whose facades still bear pockmarks from artillery shells. In the midst of Dresden's splendor stand the ruins of a church, the "Frauenkirche." This stone rubble, along with Kurt Vonnegut's *Slaughterhouse Five*, is perhaps the best reminder of the Allied firebombing that leveled much of the city and killed 35,000 in 1945.

Almost immediately after Germany was divided by the Allies in 1945, the eastern part became—because of its economic inferiority and political repression—the unfortunate sibling of the two. This legacy, which has imprinted itself in people's minds and psyches, continues in a period of persistent economic inequality. The open wall has revealed the political and economic bankruptcy of East Germany. Almost overnight, West German firms descended on the eastern regions, which represented a huge new market. Predictably, they have profited immensely from unification. But the "economic miracle" that East Germans expected to follow the currency union in 1990 is behind schedule as politicians agree that painful sacrifice lies ahead in a difficult transition period.

The region's antiquated infrastructure—which you will encounter if you try to phone home—and unresolved property ownership issues—a consequence of unification—have deterred Western businesses from making capital investments. As a consequence, East

Germans are faced with skyrocketing prices, unemployment, and diminishing social services.

East German culture—the institutions as well as producers and products—is also vanishing. Few East German newspapers or publishing houses have survived the marketing push of large, successful West German enterprises. Television and radio stations, which played a pivotal role in hastening the downfall of the regime, have already merged with their powerful Western counterparts, with hundreds of employees being laid off in the process.

The coexistence of economic opportunity and social hardship may be all too familiar to the Western tourist, but for East Germans, these are bewildering phenomena, not at all what they anticipated when they revolted against their Communist regime in 1989. Far from having become equal to their glitzy Western siblings, East Germans still feel "less advantaged." Their initial euphoria over toppling a repressive regime has given way to disappointment and disillusion.

Optimistic observers talk of an inevitable period of transition and predict that five years from now the stark socioeconomic differences between East and West will have disappeared. Pessimists predict 50 percent unemployment, social dislocation, and rising alcohol consumption and ask about the enduring political and social consequences of inequality. Such factors, incidentally, explain why you might encounter political demonstrations and protests in the streets of the major cities like Leipzig, Berlin, or Rostock. These are not replays of 1989 but expressions of the new political freedom as well as the frustration and hardship East Germans are encountering both economically and psychologically. Traveling through this region you'll find the German political drama poses questions central to the new European order. Can democracy do what communism couldn't for the people of Eastern Germany? Where will the haves and have nots find common ground? And equally important, how many marks does it take to bury Marxism?

ARRIVAL

Germany is easily reached from all of Europe's major cities. Here are some of your options.

By Air: Frankfurt, the nation's principal gateway, offers easy air and rail connections to Berlin and Dresden. It is often the first choice of travelers to Germany because many discounted airfares are available to this hub. But you may find it worth spending extra for a direct flight to Berlin.

By Rail: Because of heavy construction and numerous delays on Hitler's pioneer autobahns in eastern Germany, this is our preferred method of travel within the old German Democratic Republic. You will appreciate the convenience of train links between Berlin, Dresden, and Weimar. A German Rail Pass may be your best bet if you expect to be doing a good deal of travel within the country, east and west. Sitting comfortably in a dining car and sipping coffee while surveying the countryside is still the most civilized way to travel in Germany. And when you return to your compartment, you might find your fellow travelers eager to provide inside information about their country. Many East Germans speak English well and are happy to help. If you're traveling overnight, we recommend booking a couchette.

By Car: Nowhere are the differences between the old and new Germany more apparent than on the highway. In the West, people drive fast and furious, and the absence of freeway speed limits makes life on the road difficult. In the East, construction delays will slow your pace. Of course, if you're eager to take back roads and sample village life, an automobile will be an asset. Unleaded gas is available throughout eastern Germany. But your best bet may be to use trains within Germany and then rent a car in Berlin or Dresden to proceed to Poland or Czechoslovakia.

Transit: Although eastern Germany's public transit system seems dated when compared to that of western Germany, it is efficient. You can easily get around in all towns and cities by bus or tram.

MONEY

The deutsche mark (DM) is worth $ 0.60. For a quick mental conversion from deutsche marks to dollars, multiply the German value by 6 and move the decimal point one place to the left. For example, 10 DM are worth about $6.00.

TELEPHONE

As with all calls from the United States, you must first dial 011 for international long distance, then (37) for the eastern part of the nation, followed by the local city code and number. City codes relevant to German cities in this book are Berlin (2), Dresden (51), and Weimar (621). For example, to reach 3764523 in Berlin, dial 011-37-2-3764523. Making calls to or within eastern Germany, particularly to the smaller towns, is difficult. The best time to get through is nonbusiness hours. The best way to call the United States is through USA Direct. To access this service, dial 0130-0010. An American operator will put your call through. It is best to have an operator at your hotel make the local call. Try to phone during off-peak hours. Western Germany has much better telephone service than the East.

LODGING AND FOOD

All German cities and towns are extremely safe by American standards. East Germany's largest cities boast comfortable, even luxurious, hotels and a good selection of restaurants as well as bars and cafés. Still, international tourism was not a priority for the Communist government. Last-minute hotel accommodations can be difficult to find, particularly in peak season. Fortunately, a thriving new bed-and-breakfast industry (Zimmer Frei signs are popping up across the East) has emerged to meet the new demand. They are found in big cities, small towns, and the countryside. Of course, it always makes sense to book your room as early in the day as possible if you are traveling without advance reservations.

Every town has its Stadtinformation or Fremdenverkehrsamt (tourist information offices) that will furnish you with maps, addresses of hotels and pensions, bus schedules, and other helpful advice. Youth hostels and campsites are also available throughout eastern Germany, and these can be booked in advance by contacting the local Stadtinformation office. Keep in mind that the Berlin information offices, such as the one at the train station, are open evenings. But the smaller offices in Dresden and Weimar are not. If possible, try to arrive during regular business hours when it is much easier to arrange accommodations.

HELPFUL HINTS

Local *Reisebüros* (travel bureaus) are your best bet for booking tickets for sightseeing tours, excursions, and theaters.

Students are treated well in Germany. All museums and most cultural events offer student rates and accept international student I.D. cards as evidence of student status.

Germany is a great place to shop, but keep in mind that all stores close between 6:00 and 6:30 p.m. on weekdays, at 2:00 p.m. on Saturdays, and all day on Sundays and holidays (except, of course, for flea markets). Many bakeries open their doors between 2:00 p.m. and 4:00 p.m. on Sundays to supply Germans with the freshly baked Kuchen they need to go with their afternoon Kaffee.

Berlin and Beyond

Germany's new capital, the setting for spy thrillers and movies of intrigue, is a microcosm of the larger Germany. About 750 years old, Berlin sprawls 892 square kilometers and consists of 21 independently administered districts, most of them with their own town hall and market square. Each was originally a separate town or village gradually incorporated into the metropolitan area.

When the Allies divided the defeated Germany in 1945, they carved up Berlin, the capital of the Third Reich, according to a similar scheme. The Berlin Blockade in 1947 brought West Berlin's special position as a city encircled by communism to international consciousness. And the wall, built in 1961, made Berlin the quintessential hot spot of the Cold War. In post-wall Germany, the two unequal halves of the city have begun to mend. But it will take years for this process to be complete, and every Berlin district will still retain its distinct identity. This, of course, is a bonanza for the visi-

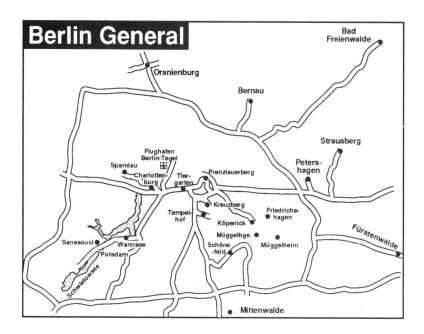

tor who wants to see the distinct and fascinating cultures of this glorious and troubled city.

From Paris to Tokyo, world capitals seem to have their decades when the whole world revolves around them. In the 1920s, Berlin was the hub of the international wheel. "New York is our suburb," quipped self-confident Berliners, who experienced a new politics, cultural experimentation, social upheaval, and economic fluctuation all rolled up into one giddy—and ultimately tragic—era. Berlin appears to once again be at center stage on the international scene. The tumbling wall signaled its rebirth, and Berlin is claiming the 1990s for itself. Although Brussels is the political and administrative seat of the new European order, Berlin captures its spirit. Here, East and West come together. But Berlin reaches beyond Europe: it is also the place where North collides with South, wealth with poverty. Refugees from Third World countries and from Eastern Europe are creating niches for themselves, giving Berlin a multi-ethnic culture very different from the homogeneity characterizing smaller German towns.

If you can make only one stop in the Federal Republic, choose Berlin. The Communist interlude, its status as headquarters of Hitler's Third Reich, the rollicking life of the gay twentys, the pomp and representation of the Prussian capital city—all have left their imprint. Its new international status has brought with it a whole new set of problems and opportunities. With its windows to the past and the future, its thriving art and entertainment scene, its vast network of parks and lakes, and its two political cultures, Berlin is simply electrifying.

Until November 1989, a fortified, well-guarded border separated the city into two unequal halves, severing two sides of a street, dead-ending trolley lines and train tracks, ripping families apart. The wall, which came to symbolize the Cold War, was Berlin's most distinctive feature until its dismantling in 1990. While Communist dignitaries visiting the East ignored its existence, Western politicians, who paid frequent calls to West Berlin—"the island of freedom in the Communist sea"—loved using the fortified border as a backdrop for their passionate speeches. Who among us could ever forget the day when German tourist John F. Kennedy notified the world that he, too, was a "Berliner."

Though it fundamentally changed the city's two halves, the wall had different consequences for East and West. West Berlin, completely surrounded by the wall, was connected to West Germany only via freeways and air routes. Its island status gave it a distinct mood and atmosphere. Residents, who felt anything but besieged, took pride in their city's special position. Padded by Bonn's seemingly endless generosity, West Berlin became a showcase for West Germany's legendary economic miracle. Cultural life in the walled city thrived. West Berlin became a favorite getaway for weekend tourists who yearned for cosmopolitan fare and flair. Berlin's heterogeneous population—native Berliners well known for their pragmatism and caustic sense of humor, Germans from all over the republic who were attracted by the city's reputation or absence of the military draft, soldiers of the American, British, and French occupying powers, and foreign workers from Italy, Yugoslavia, and Turkey (Berlin is said to be the third largest Turkish city in the world)—added an international dimension to its already legendary reputation long before the wall came down. When it did tumble,

residents accustomed to living on this "remote island" complained
—about traffic congestion and overcrowding.

East Berlin, the capital of the German Democratic Republic,
became its political, economic, and administrative center. Compared to West Berlin, it was homogeneous. Though it was by far the
wealthiest of all East German cities, it appeared poor. And though
it had more shops and goods than any other East German town and
an impressive array of cultural programs, it seemed bland compared
to its Western sibling. For anyone who could see beyond its dressed-
down gray facade, however, East Berlin held the charms of any cosmopolitan city, though less exotically packaged.

Both sides of the wall were a favored spot for Western travelers,
who were lured there by the gruesomely absurd border itself. The
West was known for its avant-garde culture and great night life, for
its theater, music, bars, and cafés, its shopping venues, and its unique
political scene. The East was visited for a "taste of socialism." Both
Berlins were home to those at the margins of mainstream life, bud-
ding artists and would-be literati, punks and squatters, students and
aspiring actors, gays and lesbians, dissidents of various persuasions.
When the wall fell on November 9, 1989, different subcultures from
the East were drawn magnetically to their Western counterparts:
middle-class families thronged through the downtown department
stores, dissidents flooded the "alternative" bars of Kreuzberg, musicians descended on jazz clubs. The fact that the social scenes tran-
scended the wall explains why a neighborhood like Prenzlauer Berg
in the East is more like Kreuzberg in the West than like the adjacent
middle-class Weissensee.

Berlin will merge more quickly than the rest of Germany, but
the long-standing differences, inequalities, and rivalries between the
two parts have left their traces. Though united, the city still falls into
two unequal halves, in part because the postwar division cemented
already existing differences. The West had always been defined by
its bars, cafés, and shops, while the East had the stiffer, more pompous civic buildings of the city. The old city center was completely
destroyed by bombing raids even before it was dissected by the wall.
Until this district is restored, the Brandenburg Gate serves as a sym-
bolic stand-in. Measured by liveliness, the city's center lies not in
the middle but in the West. West Berlin is still the more seductive of

Kurfürstendamm, the heart of Berlin (Photo by Michael Brodersen. Courtesy InterMarketing Berlin)

the two parts. But that's because most visitors to East Berlin limit themselves to its famed museums and miss its heart, some of the most fascinating and historic urban neighborhoods in Europe.

If you have not visited Berlin in the last five or ten years, you will be astonished by the transformation it has undergone since the wall fell. If you are visiting for the first time, you might be overwhelmed by the possibilities. Do you want to take a stroll through history, visiting the Empire or tracing the Third Reich, inside museum walls and beyond? Are you inclined toward the arts, galleries, exhibits? Do you fancy music or theater? Are you eager to browse in boutiques and specialty shops? Do you track down gourmet delights and connoisseur wines in every city you visit? Is it people you want to watch? Do expeditions through the "concrete jungle" excite you? Or is your taste for a more leisurely pace, around Berlin's famed waterways, parks, and forests? Whatever your notion of a great city vacation, Berlin will make it reality.

GETTING AROUND

Berlin has two airports. You will arrive at Tegel, to the north of the city. From here, you can take bus #109, which ends at Zoo Station (Zoologischer Garten), only a few steps from the Tourist Office. Plenty of taxis are also available, but this bus is very convenient to all downtown locations.

Trains also arrive at Zoo Station. Here, all public transport lines (except for the trams that service only the eastern part of the city) intersect: the subway (U-Bahn), the city train that runs above-ground (S-Bahn), and the buses. If you plan to make several trips in a single day, buy a day ticket, which allows unlimited travel on this unified Berlin network. The city's public transit system is exemplary. If you want to go door to door, taxis are much cheaper than a rental car—and always readily available.

If you are at a bar past 1:00 a.m. when subways and most buses have their "last call" on weekends, you can choose between taxis or the #119 bus. The "Nachtbus" (night bus, as it is colloquially called) usually carries a diverse crowd: animated conversations on one side and slurred speech on the other, a woman with streaked make-up behind you, a man with glazed eyes holding himself in the aisle, lovers collapsed in each other's arms, and, of course, silent couples. This is the down side of the night on the town that is invisible in America's cities where everyone heads home in cars.

With its expanded network of bicycle paths, Berlin is a great city for cyclists, and you do not have to be a great athlete to make your way around town. Except during rush hour, you can transport the bikes on the U-Bahn and the S-Bahn and leisurely explore a specific neighborhood. The **Fahhradbüro Berlin** near Kleistpark rents bicycles for 10 DM ($6) per day (#146 Hauptstr., U-Bahn, tel. 784/5562).

If you are interested in taking a boat trip along the city's irregular grid of rivers and canals, call 693/4646 for schedules and routes. Although these rides go right through the center of Berlin, they offer an amazingly quiet vantage point for some of the city's best-known as well as many "secret" sights (April to October).

LODGING

Make your hotel reservations in advance, especially if you visit during the holidays or peak summer season. You can begin planning

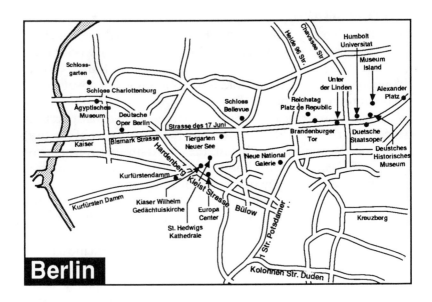

your trip to Berlin by calling 1-800-248-9539, a free information service in the United States for the Berlin bound. Within a few weeks, you will receive an information packet that includes hotels, history, cultural events, and a current schedule of events.

To find last-minute accommodations, information about excursions, brochures, and schedules for all cultural events, visit the **tourist office**, which has two downtown locations, one at the Zoo Station, open daily 8:00 a.m. to 11:00 p.m. (tel. 313/9063), and the other at nearby Europa Center, open 8:00 a.m. to 11:00 p.m. (tel. 262/6031). The **Informationszentrum** located close by at #20 Hardenbergstrasse also has general information available, free of charge. It is open Monday through Friday 8:00 a.m. to 7:00 p.m., and Saturday 8:00 a.m. to 4:00 p.m. Tel. 310/040.

For top-of-the-line accommodations in western Berlin, you cannot beat the legendary **Bristol Kempinsky**, located in the heart of the West, on Kurfürstendamm. Doubles with bath start at 280 DM ($175). South of the Kempinsky at #10 Meineckestrasse is another large first-class hotel, the **Hotel Meinicke**, which has single rooms, including a plentiful breakfast, starting around 105 DM ($65). Tel. 882/8111.

If you want to stay near Kurfürstendamm, try the **Hotelpension Aarona**, at #32 Bleibtreustrasse, where rooms range from 64 DM ($40) for a single to 96 DM ($60) for a double. Tel. 881/6274 or 881/1818. For pleasant luxury near the Adenauerplatz, stay at the **Hotel Bogota**, #45 Schlüterstrasse. Singles range from 48 DM to 96 DM ($30 to $60). Near a nice inner city park and lake, the **Hotelpension Lietzensee**, at #14 Neue Kantstrasse, with singles starting at 48 DM ($30), is an easy bus ride from the heart of East Berlin. For a slight touch of decadence, try the **Pension am Savignyplatz**, #52 Grolmanstrase, which lets you sleep in the midst of Savignyplatz nightlife. Room prices range from 40 DM to 72 DM ($25 to $45). Tel. 313/8392.

Away from the city center, you might want to try **Hotelpension Alster** located at #10 Eisenacherstrase near Winterfeldplatz, another major nightlife scene. Singles start at 48 DM ($30), a good price for its quiet back street location. Tel. 246/952. If you have a car, you might prefer the **Hotelpension Haus Trinitatis**, #62 Inchenallee, on the city's far west side. Nearby lakes and woods can make this hotel a vacation within your vacation. Rooms start at 56 DM ($35). Tel. 365/4262. West Berlin also has a women-only hotel that is definitely a cut above the YWCA. Heavily booked, the **Hotel Artemisia** is a pleasant place to stay in Berlin. It is centrally located at #18 Brandenburgische Strasse. Single rooms start at 80 DM ($50). Tel. 878/905.

Hotels in the East tend to have Western prices and Eastern quality — not necessarily a good value. Still, if you want to know what Berlin feels like from its "other side," it is essential to spend at least one night here. If price is no object, follow the lead of Japanese and West German business people who work in the East from the luxury of the **Grand Hotel**, located at #158-164 Friedrichsstrasse, at the intersection of Unter den Linden. The Communist regime built it as a prestige object designed to lure the wealthy away from the first-class hotels of the West. This modern hotel boasts all the luxuries of "Western Decadence," including marble swimming pools and saunas. The cost of its rooms — 288 DM ($180) for a single and 320 DM ($200) for a double — is almost prohibitive, but if you like a state-of-the-art hotel, you will be pleased.

Throughout Berlin, east and west, pensions are, as a rule, less expensive than hotels, usually lack none of the comfort, and provide a friendlier atmosphere. They also may be your refuge when the hotels are full. If you prefer the homey feeling of a room in a private home or apartment, consult the bed-and-breakfast agency run by Frau Neugebauer, #206 Wilhelm Pieck Strasse. Such rooms (Zimmer) start around 25 DM ($15) per night, and staying with a family might alleviate that feeling of being a stranger in a large city. Tel. 281/5841. Private rooms can also be arranged in eastern Berlin at the government-run **Verkehrsamt Berlin Alexanderplatz**, 0-1020 Unter dem Fernsehturm. Tel. 212/4512. In addition, *Herzlich Willkommen*, a booklet provided by Berlin tourist offices, lists other bed-and-breakfast possibilities.

In Germany, virtually all hotels and pensions have pleasant dining rooms where breakfast (included in the price of the room) is served. As you enter, you will notice the hush—occasionally interrupted by someone tapping the shell of a soft-boiled egg—of people concentrating on their first meal of the day. It is customary to say "Guten Morgen" to other patrons as you sit down. As you may know, Germans also say "Guten Tag" to no one in particular when they enter a small shop and "Auf Wiedersehen" when they leave.

Although Berlin has more than a dozen youth hostels, these do fill up during vacations and holidays, so it is best to book your stay in advance. The **Informationszentrum Berlin** mentioned at the beginning of this Lodging section can book rooms in advance, as can the **Reisebüro der FDJ** at #5 Alexanderplatz, in East Berlin. Tel. 215/3633. Book as early in the day as possible.

Berlin has four campsites, but you'll need a car to reach them conveniently. At a cost of 5 DM ($3) per tent and 6 DM ($3.60) per person, they are a bargain for those planning an extended stay. The nicest is **Camping Kladow**, located at #11-117 Krampnitzer. It can be reached by bus #35. Tel. 365/2797.

Another possibility for anyone planning to spend more than a few days in Berlin is one of several **Mitwohnzentralen**. These agencies will try to find almost any kind of room for a week or longer. The Mitwohnzentrale on the third floor of Kurfürstendamm-Eck, #227-8 Kurfürstendamm, is the largest and most centrally located of these offices. It is open Monday through Friday 10:00 a.m. to 7:00 p.m., Saturday and Sunday 11:00 a.m. to 3:00 p.m. The influx of Eastern Europeans to Berlin has made competition for available longer-term rooms quite stiff, so it is advisable to reserve a place

Neptune Fountain, Berlin (Courtesy InterMarketing Berlin)

well ahead of time. Do not expect to breeze through this office late in the day. Many of the people waiting in line are reserving for next week or next month. In peak season, the lines can be long. If you don't speak German, try to find someone waiting in line who does. Ask them to check today's availability.

FOOD

Of course, when you're in the mood for a quick bite to eat, head for a snack bar, German style, where you get various kinds of Wurst, pommes frites (french fries), and beverages (including beer). For more formal dining, you'll find a wide array of restaurants, certainly the widest in Eastern Europe. Restaurants in Berlin are plentiful and varied. Whatever your taste, you can accommodate it, often late into the evening.

In western Berlin, the **Café Einstein**, at #58 Kurfürstenstrasse, is a must for literary folks. It has a beautiful back garden and serves delightful (if pricey) Viennese food, often to live music. The **Cour Carree**, #5 Savignyplatz, is a popular French restaurant. In the center of town, it offers outdoor dining in the warm months. The **Exil** on the banks of the Landwehrkanal at #44 Paul-Lincke Ufer is a meeting place for artists, but it is too established to be trendy. The meals, also Viennese style, are superb (save room for dessert!), and the ambience is wonderful. After the war, the **Paris Bar**, #153 Kantstrasse, was the city's most famous meeting place for artists, intellectuals, and writers. High prices now attract a more upscale clientele.

Berlin probably has more Italian restaurants than Sienna, most of them run by Italian immigrants. The **Osteria** near the Viktoriapark at #71 Kreuzbergstrasse, is probably the best-known restaurant collective in the city. The food is inexpensive and good, and the atmosphere is lively.

Most East Berlin restaurants retain something of the old GDR ambience, including lines of patrons eager to be seated. Virtually all serve a version of Deutsche Küche, and menus tend to revolve around meat. For a solid meal in a patrician setting, choose the **Ermeler Haus**, at #10 Am Märkische Ufer, complete with frescoed ceilings and gilded statues. Tel. 275/5113. For the literary crowd, the **Keller Restaurant Brecht Haus**, #125 Chausseestrasse, is a must. It is located in the cellar of Bertolt Brecht's house (a small museum worth a visit), and although decorated with Brecht memorabilia, it is much too lively to feel like a shrine. This is a popular spot, so make reservations if you are not prepared to wait. Tel. 282/3848. **Restaurant Ganymed**, located near the Berliner Ensemble and Deutsches Theater at #5 Schiffbauerdamm, had an oddly mixed clientele in the days of the walled city. American and British officers and soldiers dined next to East Germans dressed up for the theater. It is an oldfashioned kind of place, with a *garderobe* where you can check your hat and aproned waiters who attend to your every need.

Berlin Café Society

Although most of the restaurants listed above also serve coffee and light snacks, including desserts, cafés are a proud European tradition ideal for a brief stop or a long pause.

In West Berlin, Kurfürstendamm shoppers who want to watch the passing scene enjoy the **Café Leysiefer**. It's located near the Ku-Damm station. The **Filmbühne**, centrally located at the corner of

Hardenbergstrasse and Steinplatz, is geared, as the name suggests, to the film crowd and offers an extensive menu. **Café Savigny**, at #53 Grolmanstrasse, is frequented by the trendy Savignyplatz crowd. In Kreuzberg, the **Café Adler**, located at #206 Friedrichstrasse, keeps alive the ghost of Checkpoint Charlie, where an entire generation of tourists, smugglers, and soldiers passed to the other side of the wall. It is a tastefully decorated place great for writing postcards and musing about the border that is no more. On the Kreuzberg itself, in the Viktoriapark, the **Golgotha** offers great outdoor seating. Often the music is loud enough to inspire dancing. And for all-nighters, there is the famous and infamous **Schwarzes Café**, located at #148 Kantstrasse. It's worth a visit just to check out the garishly coiffed, imaginatively dressed crowd.

In eastern Berlin, the café crowd tends to split into those—mostly older and more conventional—who take their Kaffee und Kuchen seriously and those who come to engage in discussions. For the former, visit the **Alt Berliner Conditorei**, Neue Schönhauser Strasse-Weinmeisterstrasse, for a fanciful selection of pastries. Or try the **Café im Palais**, #16 Poststrasse, where a violin and piano duo make indulgence an almost sentimental affair.

The Café Flair (also known as the Café Lila), #72 Stargardstrasse, is considered one of the best in the unified city. It has the ambience of an old Parisian café, and its location in the heart of Prenzlauer Berg makes it a favorite of the art crowd. **The Wiener Café**, at #68 Schönhauser Allee 68, draws a similar crowd and is also good for eavesdropping on conversations. If your German isn't up to it, crowd watching is also great entertainment. For a replica of an Old Berlin café and a diverse clientele, try the **Kaffeestube**, #1058 Husemannstrasse.

Most cafés, incidentally, serve great breakfasts. Considering the amount of time Germans spend lingering over breakfast if given the opportunity, this could be the most important meal of the day.

NIGHTLIFE

Berlin's music scene includes the well established as well as the off-beat. Opera fans will flock to the **Deutsche Oper**. An evening at the **Berlin Philharmonic Hall** is a treat regardless of the particular concert being performed because of its superlative acoustics. In addition, you will find that smaller musical events of all types are offered every evening of the week. It is the same for theater. If your taste is more for the mainstream, choose the **Schiller Theater** or the **Deutsches Theater.** The **Schaubühne** is world-famous for its superb actors and its experimental style. In Kreuzberg, you will find small avant-garde stages.

For other nightlife ideas, consult your hotel desk, the **Litfassäulen** (advertising pillars which have a long history in Berlin), or the biweekly publications, *Tip* and *Zitty*, for daily listings of events that even the non-German speaker will be able to decode.

BARS

As a rule, all restaurants, or Gaststätten, serve alcohol. In addition, Berlin has bars too numerous to count. These fall into two categories, which you will learn to distinguish by the outside decor: the publike Kneipen, which tend to cater to a working-class clientele and serious drinking, and the trendier, more clublike establishments, where patrons who want to see and be seen are more likely to sip and chat.

Berlin has more bars than any other German city. These have no legal closing time, so do not wait for "last call." On weekends, the city's main streets and boulevards will be populated, even crowded, until the morning hours, and there is nothing like watching the sun rise after a balmy summer night on the town. For such a large city, Berlin is incredibly safe even when compared to other major European cities. Though women are not free from harassment, they take walking alone after dark as a given.

SIGHTSEEING

Charting excursions through Berlin is like picking your favorite movie: as you begin to recollect, more and more possibilities flood your mind until finally it seems impossible to settle on anything. As much as possible, we organized these as walking tours, because this allows you to experience the best of Berlin at a leisurely pace, strike up a conversation with a fellow pedestrian, or stop at a local café.

The Heart of the West

Not surprisingly, the heart of "West Berlin" is its famous shopping district, downtown. At night, you will find theaters, cabarets, nightclubs, and movie houses here. For a day tour, begin at **Wittenbergplatz**, with the **KADEWE**. As long as West Berlin was the showcase of capitalism, the KADEWE with its stunning displays symbolized consumer's paradise. This department store has a quiet elegance and a grand history. On the eighth floor, you will find the "food" section. If it wasn't full of perishables, it would be a museum of people's creative ways of satisfying hunger and thirst. Its many counters and stands offer ordinary and exotic specialties, ready to eat, that will delight you.

Stroll down the **Tauentzien** toward the **Kaiser Wilhelm Gedächniskirche**, a striking juxtaposition of old and new. The shell of the original church, left standing as a memorial to the war, is flanked on two sides by a modern church tower and sanctuary, whose stained glass windows create a somber beauty inside. If the action on the Breitscheidplatz—favorite hangout for tourists, skateboarders, and spare-changers—gets to be too much, you can seek refuge here.

Bear left and you will find yourself on the legendary **Kurfürstendamm**, lined with haute couture boutiques and bookstores, antique furniture shops, Meissen porcelain galleries, and souvenir stores. There are many restaurants to choose from, and one of the famous sidewalk cafés, where one goes to see and be seen, is a must. The closer you get to the Adenauerplatz, the pricier the shopping gets, especially if you follow the small side streets to the left where you will find exquisite antiques.

The sidewalk of this boulevard offers as much entertainment as the window displays: it is wide enough to accommodate a party of eight, walking abreast, as well as vendors and "starving artists" chalking colorful imitations of Rembrandt or Gauguin on its pavement. Do yourself the favor of strolling down the Kurfürstendamm during night hours at least once. Especially on weekends, the flood of people moving along will amaze you.

From the Ku-Damm, as Berliners call it, you can turn right down Grolmanstrasse or Knesebeckstrasse to reach the Savigny-

Kurfürstendamm, Berlin (Photo Michael Brodersen. Courtesy InterMarketing Berlin)

platz's more interesting shops and cafés. The S-Bahn will take you from there to Zoo Station, Berlin's main train station, which is usually crowded with people of all nationalities. For a break from the city, continue past the station to the Tiergarten, a huge park, or visit the zoo, which first opened in the nineteenth century and had to be restocked almost completely after starving Berliners made game of its wildlife during the first poor and gruesomely cold post-war winter.

As an alternative, step onto the #119 bus at any corner of the Kurfürstendamm and head back, past Wittenbergplatz to Nollendorfplatz, which was the center of the well-established gay community in the Weimar Republic. At night, this area is lively, because of its many bars and clubs including the proto-deco Metropol Disco. But it also offers daytime attractions. See the flea market, uniquely situated in abandoned U-Bahn cars in a retired aboveground U-Bahn station.

Heading south, you will reach the **Winterfeldplatz** where Hausfrauen and spiked-hair men mingle at the splendid open-air market every Wednesday and Saturday morning. Here, you can buy anything from potatoes and Turkish bread to leggings and candles. Follow Goltzstrasse if you are interested in more antique shops, cafés, and small boutiques. You will eventually reach Eisenacher Strasse, and from there you can catch the subway to the Zoo Station.

The Heart of the East

Although the Alexanderplatz has its share of shops, the East's downtown was not built around consumerism or street life. More noticeable are the administrative and representational buildings of the Communist party, the stately structures of Old Berlin, the modern high-rise dwellings of inner city residents, and the impressive museums and monuments from various eras.

Begin your tour at the **Alexanderplatz**, easily reached by S-Bahn. This entire area was completely destroyed in the war and rebuilt according to Socialist notions of city planning. The architecture will no doubt strike you as shabby, and the square is so vast and windy that it seems to absorb pedestrians. Except for that fateful November 4, 1989, when one million protesting East Germans precipitated the downfall of the regime, the square has been a rather predictable place.

Climb the landmark **Fernsehturm**—the highest point in Berlin—to get a sense of its size and of the extent of wartime destruction. Vast areas, especially in the East, are covered with modern high-rises, replacements for prewar apartments and tenements. You may want to stop inside the stores lining the Alexanderplatz. They have all been restocked with Western goods tagged with Western prices.

As you head for Unter den Linden, you will pass the **Marienkirche**, some 600 years old, and the prewar City Hall, both built in characteristic red brick. A wonderful fountain, the **Neptunbrunnen**, makes for a cool resting place on warm summer days. From here you can see the **Marx-Engels Memorial**, which looks quite forlorn today. Crossing the Marx-Engels Forum, bear left to reach the beautifully restored **Nikoleiviertel**, home to three small museums that retell the history of Berlin. At its center stands the twin-towered Gothic **Nikoleikirche**, which houses a museum dedicated to medieval Berlin. It is located at #1020 Nikoleikirchplatz. Hours are Sunday and Monday 10:00 a.m. to 9:00 p.m., Thursday and Saturday 10:00 a.m. to 6:00 p.m., and Friday 10:00 a.m. to 4:00 p.m. Close by at #4 Poststrasse is the **Knoblauchhaus**, built in 1759. It miraculously survived the bombs to become a museum devoted to the eighteenth-century German Enlightenment. Visiting hours are Wednesday and Saturday 10:00 a.m. to 5:00 p.m., Thursday and Sunday 10:00 a.m. to 5:00 p.m., and Friday 10:00 a.m. to 4:00 p.m. If you want to trace the city's development in the nineteenth century, visit the exhibits in the newly rebuilt rococo **Ephraim Palais**, #1020 Am Mühlendamm at the intersection of Poststrasse. The Palais is open Monday 10:00 a.m. to 4:00 p.m., Tuesday and Sunday 10:00 a.m. to 5:00 p.m., and Wednesday and Saturday 10:00 a.m. to 6:00 p.m.

If you skip this detour, you will see the **Palast der Republik** facing the Marx-Engels Platz, an extremely costly, almost garish structure built by the Communists to replace the imperial palace destroyed by bombs. Cross the Marx-Engels Platz and bear right to Unter den Linden, the main artery of imperial Berlin. On the right side of the boulevard is the **Bebelplatz**, where Nazis fed hundreds of books to the flames during the infamous Bücherverbrennung on May 11, 1933.

Facing it is the **Deutsche Staatsoper**, a neoclassical building designed by the architect von Knobbelsdorff. Continue north until you reach the statue of **Frederick the Great** riding majestically on his horse. Until the Communists liberalized their view of German history in 1980 to include aristocrats and monarchs, Frederick was banished to Potsdam, where his corpse has only recently been reburied.

Cross the boulevard and head back on the other side. You will pass **Humboldt Universität**, a neoclassical structure, and architect Schinkel's most famous building, the **Neue Wache**, which used to house the Royal Watch and today stands as a memorial to the victims of fascism. Walk past the Dom to reach the **Museumsinsel** (Museum Island). The **Altes Museum** and the **National Gallery**, which have the same hours (Wednesday, Thursday, Saturday, and

Sunday 9:00 a.m. to 6:00 p.m. and Friday 10:00 a.m. to 6:00 p.m.), contain large collections of paintings and other artworks. The **Pergamon Museum** can be visited Saturday through Thursday from 9:00 a.m. to 6:00 p.m. and Friday 10:00 a.m. to 6:00 p.m. It is world-famous for its Department of Antiquities, which includes the Pergamon Altar.

From Marx-Engels Platz Station, you can take the S-Bahn directly back to Zoo Station. You will pass Friedrichstrasse Station, which used to be the border point most frequented by Berliners and Germans, the site of happy reunions and tragic separations. In those days, an innocuous-looking building stood to the right of the station, the **Tränenbunker**, or Bunker of Tears, as it was known colloquially. Its appearance camouflaged the sophisticated security and surveillance networks inside. Here, people took leave of each other before the visitors' midnight curfew and Westerners disappeared behind thick doors. In a way, this was the heart of Berlin when the wall stood, and if sidewalks could talk, these would.

The Infamous Past

This is a tour of the (visible) remnants of Germany's darkest historical era, which began in 1933, when Hitler was elected chancellor. The division of the country and the city that followed military defeat in 1945 is part of that historic chapter. East Germany and its capital East Berlin, which had their own share of horrors, are part of this political nightmare.

It seems appropriate for this tour to begin at the symbol of the reunited Germany—the **Brandenburg Gate**, built in 1791 as a triumphal arch. As you look down the broad Strasse des 17. Juni on one side and the famous Unter den Linden on the other, you'll see the pomp and splendor of imperial Germany. If you follow the course where the wall once stood, lined with plaques commemorating those who died trying to flee, you will see the **Reichstag**. Built in the nineteenth century to house the German parliament, the Reichstag was burned in 1933, which precipitated Hitler's taking control of Germany. The historical exhibit, *Questions on German History*, is a useful introduction for some of the things that follow on this tour. It is open Tuesday through Sunday from 10:00 a.m. to 5:00 p.m.

Retrace your steps toward the Brandenburger Tor, and head west to the **Soviet War Memorial**. Built from the marble of Hitler's destroyed Berlin headquarters, it is testimony to the Red Army's liberation of Berlin in 1945 and reminds us that the United States and the Soviet Union were allies before the Cold War set in. Stroll through the Brandenburg Gate (can you feel echoes of jubilation that captured people's hearts when the wall opened?) and turn right on the Grotewohl Strasse.

The spot where the land inclines to your right marks the remains of **Hitler's bunker**, where the Führer spent his last days. Continuing south, you will pass Potsdamer Platz, hub of Old Berlin. One of the dusty buildings farther on was Göring's Air Ministry. The wall used to pass right alongside it. On the other side is the **Martin Gropius Bau**, a wonderfully restored museum at #10 Stresemannstrasse, which includes large sections of the **Jewish Museum**. It is open Tuesday through Sunday from 10:00 a.m. to 6:00 p.m. Next door is a site called **The Topography of Terror**, remnants of buildings that once housed the Gestapo, the SS, and Reich Security offices. Today, you can visit an exhibition in the cellars of the Gestapo headquarters, former site of interrogation and torture. It is open daily from 10:00 a.m. to 6:00 p.m. (free admission). When you exit, you might notice the remains of the bombed out **Anhalter Bahnhof**, a onetime bustling Berlin train station where many Jewish prisoners embarked on their final journey to concentration camps.

From here, you can take a ten-minute walk along Wilhelmstrasse and Kochstrasse, the old newspaper district, to Friedrichstrasse, which was a favorite spot for flaneurs before its wartime destruction. **Checkpoint Charlie**, the border crossing point for diplomats and non-Germans, used to stand at its northern end, complete with armed guards, video cameras, invisible microphones, and all sorts of spy-thriller-come-to-life paraphernalia. Here, you will find the **Haus am Checkpoint Charlie**, Berlin's most popular museum. It is open daily from 9:00 a.m. to 10:00 p.m., and it documents the history of the wall and those who attempted to defy it.

To complete this journey into the darker side of history, you might want to visit any or all of the following sites, which are beyond the range of this walking tour. The permanent exhibition,

Buchenwald Concentration Camp Memorial near Weimar, Germany. Big building in background is the hotel; the other buildings are exhibits, restaurants, and offices.

Resistance to National Socialism, located at #14 Stauffenbergstrasse, documents the story of many groups opposed to Hitler. It is open Monday through Friday from 9:00 a.m. to 6:00 p.m. and Saturday and Sunday from 9:00 a.m. to 1:00 p.m. **The Plötzensee Prison Memorial**, located in northwest Berlin (take the #323 bus from Zoo Station to Saatwinkler Dasmm and walk from there), commemorates more than 2,500 political prisoners who were murdered here. Its execution chamber is chilling testimony to the methodical killing carried out by Nazis. From March to September, the memorial is open between 8:30 a.m. and 5:30 p.m. During the other months it closes at 4:00 p.m. The **Jewish Cemetery** in Weissensee is the most moving reminder of the large Jewish community of prewar Berlin. With more than 100,000 graves, it is one of the largest Jewish burial grounds in Europe. The grave markers give clues to that community's history. In many cases, the years and places of death show Hitler's intervention. One family grave marker, for example, indicates that its members, all Berlin natives, died in such different places as Sydney, Jerusalem, and Buchenwald.

The Splendid Past

Do not forget to pay a visit to imperial Berlin. The sprawling baroque **Schloss Charlottenburg** is located in the center of West Berlin and can be reached by bus #145 or #204. It is open Tuesday through Sunday from 9:00 a.m. to 5:00 p.m. Commissioned as a country residence by Queen Sophie Charlotte, it was expanded and modified in the eighteenth and nineteenth centuries. Karl Friedrich Schinkel, Berlin's most famous builder, finally completed it. You enter just behind the imposing statue of Friedrich Wilhelm, the Great Elector. The palace houses royal furnishings, a collection of china, and romantic paintings by Caspar David Friedrich. When you have had enough of chambers and furnishings, frieze panels and tapestries, meander through the vast palace gardens, first landscaped around 1700.

Just across the street from the Schloss, you will find four museums. The most famous of these, the **Ägyptisches Museum**, is located at #70 Schlosstrasse. It houses the world-renowned bust of **Egyptian Queen Nefertiti**. It is open Monday through Thursday from 9:00 a.m. to 5:00 p.m. and Saturday and Sunday from 10:00 a.m. to 5:00 p.m.

Schloss Charlottenburg used to be the favored pilgrimage for those searching for traces of German royalty. But now that visa restrictions have disappeared and transportation is easy, **Schloss Sans Souci** in Potsdam, some 20 kilometers southwest of the city, is serious competition. Schloss Charlottenburg and its wonderful adjacent park will not occupy an entire day, but a visit to Potsdam will.

The graceful rococo palace, **Sans Souci** (literally, Without Worry), completed in the 1740s, was built by the architect Knobelsdorf, according to sketches provided by Frederick the Great himself. Voltaire stayed here as the emperor's resident philosopher from 1750 to 1753, and you can visit his room as well as the Picture Gallery east of the palace. This palatial structure is surrounded by rushing fountains, splendid French-style gardens, and lush woods, landscaped in the English style. As you stroll along its path fantasizing meditative conversations between king and philosopher, it is easy to see how this became the enlightened Friedrich's favorite getaway.

Do not miss the **Chinesischer Pavilion**, a gilded structure that testifies to eighteenth-century German fascination with the exotic Orient. Inside, you can admire, appropriately enough, a collection of porcelain and china. You will also want to visit the Italian Renaissance **Orangerie** and the baroque **Neues Palais**, with an impressive facade adorned by nearly three hundred statues. **Schloss Cecilienhof**, a turn-of-the-century imitation of an English country house, was designed in a mock Tudor style. This castle became world-famous when Winston Churchill, Harry Truman, and Joseph Stalin met here to decide Germany's postwar fate in the Potsdam Conference. Here, you can see the original round table, flown in from Moscow, where the Potsdam Agreement was signed on August 2, 1945.

Before you return to Berlin, visit **Potsdam** itself, which has a nicely restored Fussgängerzone (pedestrian zone) lined with shops and a few cafés. And if you are a film buff, you might want to visit the Film Museum in Babelsberg, the eastern section of Potsdam. This was the site of the UFA studio, which produced German films. During the Communist period, the DEFA studio made films here for the GDR, including a number recognized in Cannes. From Babelsberg, you can return to the city center on the S-Bahn.

Old Berlin

To get a sense of Old Berlin, walk around one of two neighborhoods: **Kreuzberg** in the western part and **Prenzlauer Berg** in the eastern part of Berlin. You can easily spend an entire day in each of these districts. Both were left relatively undamaged by the war. Old tenement buildings that once housed workers, as well as the shops and small factories that employed them, are still standing.

Kreuzberg is far more up-to-date than Prenzlauer Berg, but it still has its share of Hinterhöfe (courtyards) that provide small shafts of light for the back buildings. Enter one of these buildings, pass-

Flea market, Berlin (Courtesy InterMarketing Berlin)

ing through various entries that become consecutively smaller and plainer, until you have reached the third or fourth Hinterhöfe, whose tenement walls are completely unadorned.

Prenzlauer Berg appears shabby. Buildings still bear shell marks and occasional washed-out lettering from prewar strores or advertising. Both districts are preferred by artists, punks, and "alternatives"; both have seen serious confrontations between squatters and police. Kreuzberg is the heart of the Turkish community and when you see kerchiefed women spinning wool on Mariannenplatz while their men read Turkish newspapers or when you grab slices of gyros in a storefront snackbar, you might feel like you are in another country.

Prenzlauer Berg: Take the S-Bahn to Sehnefelder Platz and follow the Sehnefeldstrasse north to the beautifully restored Kollwitzplatz, named after artist Käthe Kollwitz (where residents used to pay about $50 for a one-bedroom apartment). Between Kollwitzstrasse and Schönhauser Allee is a small Jewish cemetery and in the Hinterhöf (courtyard) of #53 Rykestrasse is the only functioning synagogue. Stroll about. Though you will find shops and cafés, look beyond the eye-catching colors and displays at the houses, the street lights, the cobblestones, the people—especially the old women whose backs are bowed by a personal history shaped by war, scarcity, and repression. Head west toward Schönhauser Allee, one of East Berlin's main shopping streets, which is a toned-down version of Kurfürstendamm.

Kreuzberg: Kreuzberg has two parts. Its eastern half, which ran up against the wall for almost thirty years, is less developed and more punky and has more Turkish residents. The western section is richer, more pleasant, and more sedate. Take bus #129 to Moritzplatz and follow the Oranienstrasse east. The shops are a mix of secondhand junk and gems, Turkish crafts, and the cutting edge. The same is true for bars and restaurants. After Heinrichplatz, turn right on Manteuffelstrasse and left on Paul-Lincke Ufer.

Follow the Landwehrkanal (canal), and when you reach the Bearwaldstrasse, turn left. Proceed to the fancier Kreuzberg, where you will find novelty shops, more secondhand stores, small galleries, and plenty of eating and drinking spots. On side streets, you'll see buildings once occupied by squatters. Even if you only have time to see part of Kreuzberg, you will sense the aura of Old Berlin. On Mehringdamm, you can catch bus #119 and head back to the Kurfürstendamm.

Green Berlin

Berlin is one of the few large cities that juxtaposes nature and civilization, stress and serenity, concrete streets and waterways. Treat yourself to a day in the green, either Western or Eastern style. I have selected only two from myriad possible "green" destinations.

The West: Take the S-Bahn to **Strandbad Wannsee**, Berlin's most famous beach, which is worth a visit on a sunny summer day, if only for the sight of serious sun-worshipers packed like sardines. You can wander for hours through the woods around Wannsee or along the river Havel. Taking an excursion on a Dampfer (a steamboat, where food and drink are served) is also a wonderful experience. Telephone 810/004 or 391/7010 for schedules, destinations, and fares. Or from 8:00 a.m. to dusk, simply take the small ferry to Pfaueninsel, a small island prohibited to cars, where a flock of peacocks strolls through the gardens of the small Schloss, built by Friedrich Wilhelm II for his mistress.

One nice thing about Germany is that wherever there is a park, a forest, or a lake, a café or restaurant is not far away. As you stroll through Grunewald (or Tiergarten), you will find a place—often with lovely outdoor seating areas—where you can refresh yourself with Berliner Weisse (a traditional alternative to beer), Kaffee und Kuchen, or Bratwurst.

The East: Take the S-Bahn to Köpenick, a sleepy suburb of Berlin with its own identity. Many factories were located in Köpenick; its working-class population might explain its resistance to national socialism. When Hitler came to power in 1933, a red flag flew from the chimney of a brewery. Take tram #84 or #96 to the Altstadt, the center of Köpenick, and walk around to get a feel for the old town. From Luisenhain opposite the Rathaus, you can take a steamboat (Weisse Flotte) to the Müggelsee, meander through its surrounding hills, called the Müggelberge, and woods. Stop for a snack at Rübezahl or Müggelseeperle. If you walk south, you will reach the Müggelturm, a tower with an observation tower, a café, a bar, and a restaurant. If you have had enough walking for the day, you can return to Köpenick by bus #27.

Weimar

Weimar is a splendid little town, a gem of German cultural history whose myriad attractions, packed densely within a small area one can easily cover by foot, will delight anyone who loves to explore the past. Weimar was virtually untouched by wartime destruction, and its core remains almost entirely the way it was when its most illustrious citizen, Johann Wolfgang von Goethe, died

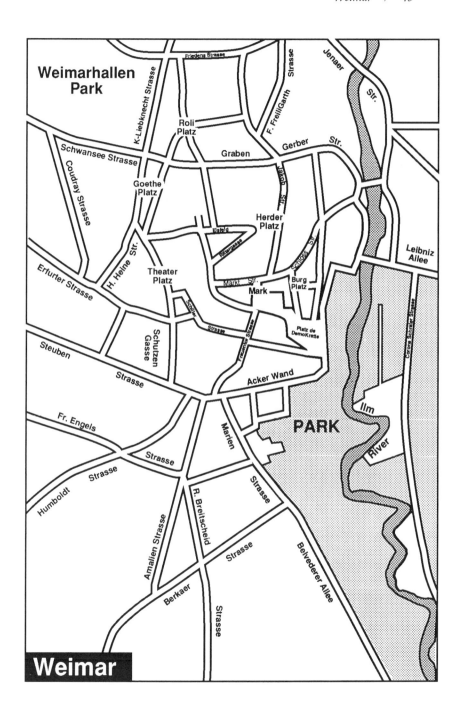

Weimarhallen Park

K-Liebknecht Strasse

Friedens Strasse

F. FreiliGarth Strasse

Jenaer

Str.

Roll Platz

Schwansee Strasse

Graben

Gerber

Str.

Coudray Strasse

Goethe Platz

Jakob Str.

Herder Platz

Leibniz Allee

H. Heine Str.

Eisfeld

Ritterpasse

Schloss Str.

Erfurter Strasse

Theater Platz

Markt Str.

Mark

Burg Platz

Steuben

Schutzen Gasse

Schiller

Strasse

Frauentor Strasse

Platz de DemoKratie

Strasse

Acker Wand

Corona Schrater Strasse

Fr. Engels

Strasse

Marien

PARK

Ilm

River

Humboldt

Strasse

Amalien Strasse

R. Breitscheid

Strasse

Belvederer Allee

Berkaer

Strasse

Strasse

Weimar

here in 1832. Egon Erwin Kisch, a German journalist well known for his biting commentary, calls Weimar "a poet's biography writ large." But there is more to it than poetry: the enlightened dukes of Saxony-Weimar, who reigned here from the seventeenth to the nineteenth century, have left their aristocratic legacy, composers Liszt and Richard Strauss resided here, Walter Gropius founded the Bauhaus here. To escape the revolutionary unrest of the capital city, the German parliament met here in 1919 to draw up the constitution of post-World War I Germany's ill-fated Weimar Republic. You may feel as though you are walking through an open-air museum as you make your way from one highlight to the next.

Although Weimar was the most popular tourist destination outside Berlin during the Communist era, it was untouched by commercialism until the currency union in the summer of 1990. Before then, everything about Weimar seemed solidly serene; even the hues of its renovated buildings seemed authentic. There was always a kind of stillness in the narrow streets and around the historic squares, Marktplatz and Theaterplatz, where people gathered in outdoor cafés or on the steps of the Schiller and Goethe monument. Low-key store window displays scarcely distracted from the beauty of facades or from the slight inclines and windings of the cobblestoned lanes. Against this background, the garish colors and slogans of consumer culture seem like intrusions. But for now, Weimar's unique beauty is stronger than such challenges.

SIGHTSEEING

If you arrive in Weimar by train, take bus #4 or #5 for a short ride to Goethe Platz. If you come by car, you will find several parking lots near the town center. No buses run in there, and car traffic is quite restricted, a blessing for pedestrians. Walk east on Geleitstrasse, to Eisfeldstrasse, until you reach the Stadtkirche St. Peter und Paul, popularly known as "Herderkirche." This church was originally built in 1249 and reconstructed after a fire ravaged it in 1424. It is an Evangelical church where services are still held regularly. In the past, Herder preached here and Bach played the organ. Today, it is best known for its altar, painted by Cranach, and its organ concerts.

Proceed east toward the Grand Ducal Palace, on the Burgplatz, which has a wonderful art collection that includes works by

Albert Schweitzer and friends, a statue in Weimar, Germany

Cranach, Veronese, and Rubens. Follow the Schlossgasse toward the market. To your left, you will see the stately Krims Krachow Haus, a Renaissance building from the early sixteenth century, whose furnishings capture the tastes of the upper class around the turn of the eighteenth century. On the right is the Tourist Information Office. You might want to linger near the fountain in the central square before continuing south down the Frauentorstrasse to visit the house of the man around whom this entire town seems to revolve: Goethe, Germany's "count of poetry."

This house, which the poet himself styled during his lifetime to be a museum after his death, is stately, almost pompous, with its exquisite furnishings and numerous collections. Highlights are Goethe's personal rooms: his sparse writing office and his spartan bed chamber, which contains nothing but a narrow bed and a chair, where his faithful male secretary Eckermann would take dictation every morning. Although Goethe loved pomp and representation, these tiny rooms attest to the fact that his mind and his creativity needed simplicity to flourish.

When you exit, retrace your steps up the Frauentorstrasse and turn left on Schillerstrasse to reach Schiller's house. This home seems quite modest compared to Goethe's, a sign of the latter's status as court poet. After a look around, return to the street for refreshment in one of the cafés. You can end your tour at the Theaterplatz, where Schiller and Goethe are commemorated in a statue that exaggerates Goethe's height.

Other spots merit a visit in Weimar. Franz Liszt's house on the Belvedere Allee is a pleasant museum that captures aspects of his life as well as his lifetime. Nearby, the site of the original Bauhaus on Geschwister Scholl Strasse is now an academy of architecture and has an exhibit open to the public. Farther south, you will find the historical cemetery on Am Posekschen Garten. It is known for the Goethe-Schiller vault, but its many old grave markers and tombstones, shadowed by beautiful willow trees, are really a foray into history. Finally, there is the English-style Park an der Ilm, planned and landscaped by Goethe. Here, you can take long strolls at night without having any second thoughts about your safety. In the middle of the park stands Goethe's first Weimar residence, the Gartenhaus, quaint and unpretentious compared to his later residence.

You do not need a car to make the most of Weimar, so if you arrive by car, park it somewhere and proceed on foot. You may want to use it to explore the city's surroundings, but the most famous sites on the outskirts of town—Schloss Tiefurt and Schloss Belvedere —are easily accessible by bus. Schloss Tiefurt, located to the east of the city, is a rococo structure built around the turn of the seventeenth century. Its lovely park, full of winding paths, fountains, summerhouses and grottoes, is the main attraction for locals, who often come here on their Sonntagsspaziergang, the traditional Sunday walk that usually ends with coffee and cake. The park is accessible by bus #3, which leaves from the Goethe Platz. As an alternative, you might want to promenade south, to Schloss Belvedere. This small palace was built between 1724 and 1732 as a hunting residence. Today it houses a rococo museum. The orangerie and pavilions located in the surrounding park merit a closer look.

Buchenwald, a former concentration camp that has been turned into a memorial site, lies to the northwest of Weimar. It is testimony to the darkest chapter of German history, and as a com-

The crematorium at Buchenwald, near Weimar, Germany

plement to Weimar's niceties, it is a must for the foreign visitor. The camp was constructed in 1937, on the Ettersberg, and it was in operation until April 11, 1945. Two days before American soldiers and tanks reached the camp, its prisoners had staged their own liberation.

During the eight years of its operation, more than 56,000 prisoners died here. Most of those murdered were Jews, but there were also many German political prisoners (most notably, the leader of the German Communist party, Ernst Thälmann) and thousands of Russian prisoners of war. It is an amazing fact of German history that a death camp like Buchenwald could exist in such close proximity to the town most famous for its enlightened culture. Of course, most Weimar residents deny having had any knowledge of the goings-on in Buchenwald.

The fact that trains full of prisoners went right through the city and chain gang convoys built and repaired roads in the area is testimony to the great power of repression. But it should be noted that Weimar never registered its opposition to the Third Reich. In 1926, Hitler held the first Party Congress (Reichsparteitag) here, and six years later, this was the first regional government consisting entirely of Nazis.

The story goes that the American soldiers occupying Thuringia requested residents of Weimar to make the long excursion to Buchenwald on foot to view the camp. Germans, old and young, male and female, could not believe the horrors they were seeing and broke down sobbing and screaming. You will feel some of what they did when you cross the mustering square (Apellplatz) or approach the camp on the "Blutstrasse" (Street of Blood), so named because the prisoners themselves had to build it under inhumane conditions that cost many of them their lives.

You can reach Buchenwald by car or with bus #L157, which departs from the train station. The memorial can be visited daily; the remainder of the camp itself and the exhibit are closed on Mondays.

LODGING

Weimar's reputation is much greater than its actual size. Only about 62,000 people reside in the town, but it is estimated that more than two and a half million visitors explore its sights every year. Still, at this point, Weimar does not have anywhere near the number of hotels one might expect. The **Hotel Elephant**, at #19 Markt, boasts a century-long list of famous visitors. Its accommodations are comfortable but not luxurious; its location, however, is perfect. On warm days, the hotel garden, where refreshments are served, is a treat. Rooms range from $45 for a single to $65 for a double. Tel. 61471, Fax 618961. The **Russischer Hof**, at #2 Goetheplatz, is a bit more expensive, with singles starting at $60 and doubles at $85. Tel. 62331. The **Hotel Thüringen**, situated across from the central train station, is great for dropping off luggage and showering after the journey, but it is a bus ride away from the attractions of the town. Its single rooms start at $40, its doubles at $60. Tel. 6375. The **Haus der Frau von Stein**, located at Ackerwand, is a small pension with reasonable rates. Its rooms start at $20. Tel. 5357.

Weimar also has several youth hostels. The largest is the **Jugendgästehaus Weimar** at #11 Erich Weinert Strasse, where $15

Theater/Kasino, Weimar, Germany

includes breakfast and $20 includes all meals. Tel. 3383. If you like camping, 10 kilometers south of town and easily accessible by car is **Oettern/Ilmtal.**

Your best bet for a homestay is to make arrangements through an office of **Weimar Information** located at Marktstrasse 3, across the hall from the main office. Hours are Monday through Friday 1:30 p.m. to 6:30 p.m., Saturday 8:30 a.m. to 1:00 p.m. Tel. 5384. Make sure that your reservation is confirmed with the host by phone.

GENERAL INFORMATION

At the tourist office **Weimar Information**, you can find out about last-minute accommodations as well as excursions and cultural events. You can also buy tickets and arrange for special guided tours through any of the museums. The office is open as follows: Monday 10:00 a.m. to 12:30 p.m., 1:30 p.m. to 6:00 p.m.; Tuesday through Friday 9:00 a.m. to 12:30 p.m., 1:30 p.m. to 6:00 p.m.; Saturday 8:30 a.m. to 1:00 p.m. Tel. 2173. A new tourist agency,

Wimare, has been operating since winter 1990. Located at Seifengasse 9, it provides essentially the same services as Weimar Information. In addition, it specializes in walking tours of the town and in putting together individual package deals according to travelers' requests. Tel. 2264.

FOOD

Weimar has numerous restaurants and cafés. Some of these are currently being renovated and expanded and will reopen for business at the end of 1991. For now, there are a number of snack bars for those who do not want to wait for a table at one of the nicer restaurants. You might also try the **Weimarhalle**, a large, fairly inexpensive establishment in the Weimarhallenpark that serves traditional Thüringer food. It is open until 11:00 p.m. and operates a beer garden during the summer. Tel. 2341. The **Ratskeller** on the Markt is a romantic wine restaurant. You must make reservations for a meal. The Chinese food served here seems a bit out of place in such a traditional German setting. Tel. 4142. The most famous of all eating establishments is the historical restaurant, **Zum Weissen Schwan**, located on the Frauenplan near Goethe's house. The cuisine is first-rate, and the setting, tasteful and intimate, befits Weimar's cultural heritage. Outside of the city proper, you can enjoy delicious Thüringer specialties at **Zum Fiaker** in Oberweimar, open until 2:00 a.m. on Friday and Saturday nights. Tel. 2848. After a walk to Belvedere, you can rest at the **Schlossgaststätte Belvedere**. On warm days, when the garden is open, dining here is a special pleasure.

If you are in the mood for coffee or ice cream, the **Café Resi**, located adjacent to the Castle on the Grüner Markt is a must. It is the favorite of students of the architectural and music schools, theater people, and artist types. The **Goethe Café**, situated at #4 Wielandstrasse on the Goetheplatz, is—as the name suggests—a more traditional place. The **Brunnenbar**, near the fountain on #11 Schillerstrasse, serves coffee specialties and ice cream. From here, you can observe the pedestrian zone "Esplanade"; on warm days, you can sit outside.

Dresden

D resden has always been known as the "Florence on the Elbe River," both for its art treasures and its architecture. If you arrive by train and begin walking down Prager Strasse toward the world-famous Altstadt, however, you might fear that you disembarked at the wrong station. Nothing you see will even remotely resemble what the city's reputation promises. Today, Dresden is a city of opposites: eighteenth-century splendor and riches contrast with harrowing stone skeletons mutely testifying to the ravages of World War II. Dismal-looking rows of GDR-style apartment buildings stand alongside Western-style luxury shops and boutiques. Most visitors come to see the art and the opera, the gems and the porcelain, but the city's less lofty and darker sights deepen its character and keep it from being a mere fairy tale place.

Socialist realism is probably the first thing you'll notice in Dresden. Blocks of *Plattenbau*, relentlessly shabby prefab high-rises, which could be called misfits of modern architecture if they did not fill street after street, surround Dresden's treasures on three sides. Though they are less sensational than the famous ruin of the Frauenkirche, they, too, testify to the destruction of Dresden in the last weeks of war. If the city's most populated area had not been fire-bombed on February 13, 1945—a date still remembered every year when the city's church bells toll their lament for fifteen minutes— the postwar regime would have been able to allocate its scarce resources differently. What makes the Frauenkirche memorial so spectacular is that it has not been "cleaned up" like the Kaiser Wilhelm Gedächtnis Kirche in Berlin. At this point, what is left of the baroque church is a gaping ruin, traces of molten stone, and heaps of rubble overgrown by weeds.

Across from the Frauenkirche ruin on the Neumarkt you will see the remains of the palace of Saxony's kings, which is currently being restored. The other splendors of old Dresden—the **Zwinger**, the **Albertinum**, and the **Semper Opera House**—have all been painstakingly restored from old drawings and photographs. These, together with the riverside promenade called the **Brühlsche Ter-**

rassen, are the heart of "Saxon baroque." All embody the legacy of King August I, who ruled Saxony in the eighteenth century.

What Goethe is to Weimar, "August the Strong," as the king was popularly known, is to Dresden. Besides conducting routine matters of state, August filled the buildings constructed for him with precious items he avidly collected. He led wars against Poland and still had time to produce more than three hundred children—only one of whom was legitimate. He is so identified with the city that even in the early years of socialism when royalty was officially shunned as "absolutist decadence," August's brilliantly gilded statue on the Neustädter Markt was one of the city's landmarks. Still, the old Communists made no secret of their disapproval. In the official GDR guidebook to August's hunting castle, Moritzburg, located on the outskirts of Dresden, a description of August's extravagant life-style ended with the sentence, "Today we regard such doings as vices and excesses of the absolutist royal court." Such admonitions disappeared with the wall, and today you can enjoy August's legacy without guilt.

If you have less than a day available for sightseeing, you might find the museums overwhelming because they contain so much that is breathtakingly beautiful. The **Zwinger**, paragon of the Saxon baroque style, was originally built by architect Matthias Daniel Pöppelman. Although it was used in the early eighteenth century for court festivities, it was not completed until the middle of the nineteenth century. The Zwinger is lavishly decorated with statuary, fountains, and the nymph baths.

The Zwinger's famous Old Masters collection, which includes Raphael's **Sistine Madonna** and works by Rubens, Rembrandt, Dürer, Titian, and others, has been transferred to the Albertinum while the Old Wing is being renovated. But there is the Mathematics and Physics Salon, which houses old tools for discovery, experimentation, and movement. The most popular exhibit in the Zwinger traces Dresden's most famous tale of experimentation: the European discovery of porcelain by Johann Friedrich Böttger, an alchemist who was imprisoned by August I and ordered to manufacture gold. Böttger succeeded in making what came to be called "white gold," and the Porcelain Collection, one of the world's greatest, exhibits masterpieces of this art. After seeing these exqui-

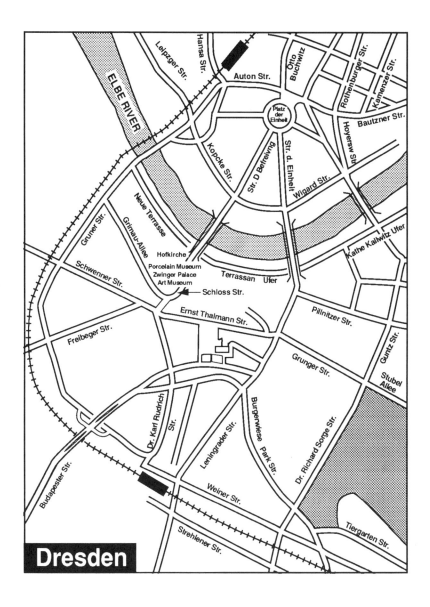

Dresden

sitely beautiful pieces, most of which were made for use as well as for show, you may never want to drink from a plastic mug again. The Zwinger is open Monday through Thursday and Saturday and Sunday, from 9:00 a.m. to 5:00 p.m. Tel. 484-0127.

The most fanciful items in Dresden (perhaps in all of eastern Germany), the treasures of the "Green Vault," are on view at the **Albertinum Museum**. The Grünes Gewölbe is named after the green walls of the strongroom of Dresden's old royal castle, which was first opened to the public as a museum of courtly riches in 1730. Compared to these intricate, playful creations—miniature "toys" made of gold, ivory, diamonds, and gems of all sorts—the Crown jewels of London seem bombastic and staid. These are fairy tale figurines and trinkets that beckon you to reach out and touch, to look more closely. Alas, that is *Verboten*, of course! Enter the Albertinum at the Georg Treu Platz on Monday, Tuesday, Friday, Saturday, and Sunday from 9:00 a.m. to 5:00 p.m. Tel. 495-3056.

Nothing can compete with these preciosa, unless you are lucky enough to meet with brilliant sunlight outside. But do have a look at the New Masters Gallery before you leave the Albertinum. It has an impressive collection that includes C. D. Friedrich, Menzel, van Gogh, and various impressionists as well as GDR artists. To see this exhibit, enter the Albertinum at Brühlsche Terrasse on Tuesday and Thursday through Sunday from 8:00 a.m. to 5:00 p.m. It is open on Wednesday from 9:00 a.m. to 6:00 p.m. Tel. 495-3056. How did all of these works of art survive the war? They were hidden in cellars, buried underground, and retrieved long after the bombing raids had stopped.

Dresden has its own art academy, and for that reason alone, not all of its art is contained in museums. Throughout the Communist era, one private gallery, the **Kühl Gallery** located in Neustädt, managed to survive. In these post-wall times, it is bound to flourish as a window to the future of art in united Germany.

The **Semperoper** is one of the most famous theater structures in all of Europe. Located at #2 Theaterplatz, it was first built in the mid-nineteenth century by Gottfried Semper in the High Renaissance style, and its lavish interior is worth a tour. If you can manage to get opera tickets, see the inside of the Semperoper at night. A daytime visit is cold compared to the festive extravagant atmosphere that reigns during evening performances. Tel. 484-2491.

Frauenkirche, Dresden, a memorial to the bombing of Dresden during World War II

The Elbe River borders the Altstadt on one side. Dresden's fans have argued for decades over which riverbank affords a more breathtaking view of the city. If you promenade down the Brühlsche Terrassen, you enjoy a view of the grasslands on the Neustädter banks of the Elbe River; from that side, you can see the Terrassen as well as the famed panorama of the Old City's baroque buildings and churches. Decide for yourself. Cross the city's oldest bridge, named after Georgi Dimitroff, and you will reach the golden statue of August the Strong on the Neustädter Markt. From there, you can stroll down the Strasse der Befreiung, the city's second large pedestrian zone. Because it is lined with old and new houses and shaded by large trees, it is much more pleasant than the Prager Strasse. But don't forget to cast a glance across the river, to see if you agree that this is the more splendid view.

Before you leave Dresden, consider one or all of the following sites outside of the city proper. The baroque **Schloss Moritzburg**, King August's hunting castle, is beautifully situated on a small island in a serene landscape of ponds and meadows and trees. It is open Tuesday through Sunday from 10:00 a.m. to 5:00 p.m. Tel. 0297-439. The journey is a treat in itself. From the Postplatz in Dresden, take tram #4 or #5 to Radebeul, a suburb of Dresden. At the train station, Radebeul-Ost, a small steam train called Sächsische Schmalspurbahn runs up the Elbe River banks to the castle, which is filled with porcelain, hunting paraphernalia, and other artifacts of August's life.

On your return to the Radebeul train station, do walk the short distance to the **Villa Shatterhand** in Karl May Strasse 5. This is a museum to Karl May, one of Germany's most famous (and influential) authors who remains virtually unknown outside of his homeland. In the nineteenth century, May wrote scores of adventure books about the rugged Wild West and the exotic Middle East, without ever having seen any of the places he brought to life for generations of German youngsters. His descriptions of American Indians as courageous and noble savages threatened by the "White Man" shaped the collective German idea of "America" more incisively than factual history books. For this reason alone, it is worthwhile to visit the Karl May Museum. It is open daily from 9:00 a.m. to 5:00 p.m. Tel.74-630.

Finally, of course, there is Meissen, a beautiful medieval town, world-famous for its porcelain factory. At the **Staatliche Porzellan-**

Steam train near Dresden, Germany

manufaktur, located on Leninplatz 9, you can visit the large porcelain exhibit, consisting of more than 3,500 pieces. But the demon-
stration workshop, where you can watch skillful molders and
painters in various stages of the manufacturing process, is probably
of greater interest to connoisseurs of "white gold." It is open from
Tuesday through Sunday, 8:30 a.m. to noon and 1:00 p.m. to 4:30
p.m. Those who saw enough porcelain in the Zwinger Museum
will still enjoy a walk through this charming town, which offers,
among its many treasures, an imposing Gothic **cathedral** and the
Albrechtsburg, which exemplifies the transition from fortified castle to representational palace. Although the town center is closed to
automobiles, parking lots are nearby. You can easily reach Meissen
by S-Bahn or, during the summer (April-October), via one of the
steamboats of the Weisse Flotte. Tel. 437-241.

LODGING

Dresden's tourist bureau, **Informationszentrum,** has two locations
and offers many services. In addition to arranging accommodations
(including homestays), it provides information on cultural events

Dresden, Zwinger Museum on the left

and excursions, sells tickets for most events, and organizes individual and group sightseeing tours. The main office at #8010 Prager Strasse is open Monday through Friday from 9:00 a.m. to 8:00 p.m. and Saturday and Sunday from 9:00 a.m. to 1:00 p.m. Tel. 495-5025; Fax 495-1276. The second location at Neustädter Markt is open Monday through Friday from 9:00 a.m. to 6:00 p.m. and Saturday and Sunday from 9:00 a.m. to 4:00 p.m. Tel. 53-539.

If you like luxury accommodations, you have a choice of either bank of the Elbe—a difficult choice. The **Hotel Bellevue**, situated at #15 Köpckestrasse on the "other side" of the river, is an Old World hotel that offers a great view of Dresden's famous skyline. Tel. 56-620; Fax 55-997. **Hotel Dresdner Hof** is a modern first-class hotel in the center of the Altstadt, at #5 An der Frauenkirche. Tel. 48-410; Fax 484-1700. Both have steep prices, ranging from 350 to 420 DM ($213 to $253). Not quite as luxurious is the modern **Hotel Newa** at Leningrader Strasse, between the central train station and the Altstadt. Rooms range from 200 to 270 DM ($118 to $166). Tel 496-7112; Fax 495-5137. All three of these hotels have very good restaurants, and as a hotel guest, you can avoid the lines that still seem to materialize everywhere that good food is served in the eastern part of Germany.

A number of old-fashioned, reasonably priced Pensionen can be found on the Weisser Hirsch in a residential section near the Waldpark. If you like the idea of staying in a turn-of-the-century villa, try the **Pension Geier**, #45 Plattleite (tel. 36483), or the **Pension Steiner**, #49 Plattleite (tel. 36205). The adjacent **Pension Sonneneck**, #43 Plattleite (tel. 36430), has the advantage, on those rare warm mornings, of serving breakfast in a garden.

Of course, youth hostels are cheaper still. Dresden has one located at #11 Hübnerstrasse (tel. 470-667), and you will find another in Radebeul, at #12 Weintraubenstrasse. There are several camp sites in the vicinity, for example, the **Campingplatz Moritzburg, Am Mittelteichbad**. Tel. 442. But one site is actually situated in the city and has a swimming pool to boot: **Campingplatz Mockritz**, #8 Boderitzer Strasse. Tel. 478-226.

FOOD

Restaurants

The **Opernrestaurant** at #2 Theaterplatz is worth a visit simply because of its location in the middle of the Altstadt; on nice days, you can enjoy your traditional German dishes, or just a Kaffee und Kuchen, outdoors. Tel. 484-2500. On the Neustädter side of the Elbe, try the **Kügelnhaus und Neustädter Grill**, tel. 52791, or the **Äberlausitzer Töppel**, tel. 55605, on the Strasse der Befreiung #13 and #14, respectively, for Saxon specialties.

Dresden has traditionally been known for its beer and the wine that is produced by small vineyards in the surrounding area. Its beer and wine restaurants, therefore, are an essential part of the city's culinary scene. If you like beer, visit the **Bierkeller im Kügelgenhaus**, #13 Strasse der Befreiung, for a historic atmosphere (tel. 52791) or the **Radeberger Keller** for a more traditional, sometimes rowdy mood (tel. 4951281). For those who want to sample the local wines, the **Meissner Weinkeller** in the Neustädter City Hall, #1b Strasse der Befreiung, has the largest selection. Tel. 555-5814.

Cafés

If you like luxurious atmosphere, visit either **Café Pöppelmann** in the Hotel Bellevue (tel. 53425) or the **Café Vis-à-Vis** in the Dresdner Hof, Brühlsche Terrasse. Tel. 48410. During the summer months, you can sit directly on what is known as "Europe's balcony" with a wonderful view of the Elbe and Dresden Neustädt beyond. Anyone interested in literature must visit the **Café Kästner**, close to the house where writer Erich Kästner was born on Alaunstrasse 1. Although Kästner was a serious writer whose books were burned and banned under Hitler, he is best known in this country for the juvenile books, such as *Emil and the Detectives*, that he wrote under a pseudonym to avoid persecution by the Nazis. This café has a pleasant 1920s ambience. Tel. 570-445. **Café Christian** at #27b Bautzner Strasse has a small gallery exhibiting works from local artists. Tel. 55751. Finally, the **Café Toskana** at #1 Schillerplatz is famous among locals for its *gateau* and cake specialties. Tel. 30744.

Czechoslovakia

A trip to Czechoslovakia is more than just a chance to see its splendid parks and monuments, museums and concert halls, and fine restaurants and cafés. As you explore the art nouveau streets and Roman fortresses, you are likely to find yourself the object of considerable curiosity. As a Westerner, you are the window on the place most East Europeans have dreamed of visiting.

Of all the emancipated Eastern Bloc countries, Czechoslovakia is perhaps the most remarkable example of what freedom means to a nation that has spent centuries under the thumb of colonial powers. Now that the curtain has fallen on the reign of the Hapsburgs, Nazis, and Communists, the people of Czechoslovakia can create a state in their own image. Except for one brief interlude between the two World Wars, democracy has been an idea limited to political science courses.

As you explore this country, you will want to allow time to talk with your hosts in private homes and with museum guides, students, academics, and, of course, former Communists. As tourists, we like to think we are on vacation. But there is something special here, a story so absorbing that it competes favorably with the romantic landscapes and picturesque castles. In a nation that appears to have been designed by whimsical architects and color coordinated by impressionists, it is quite possible to fall in love at least once a day. And on our Great Cities route, perhaps the most compelling sights of all are the ones you least expect. Just when you have come to know this rich and varied country, you will turn a corner and find another delightful surprise that throws you off schedule, again.

Some of the finds in this chapter were not discovered on carefully plotted itineraries but on serendipitous encounters, with one

Czechoslovakia

discovery leading to the next. For example, I remember the morning in Prague I was on the telephone to a government environmental official. He would be delighted to see me. There was just one problem. He happened to be at his home in Banská Bystrica, 200 miles away in Slovakia. That journey, which took me through some of the impressive cities described here, was unforgettable. Great medieval towns and castles, quaint cobblestone streets, and monumental

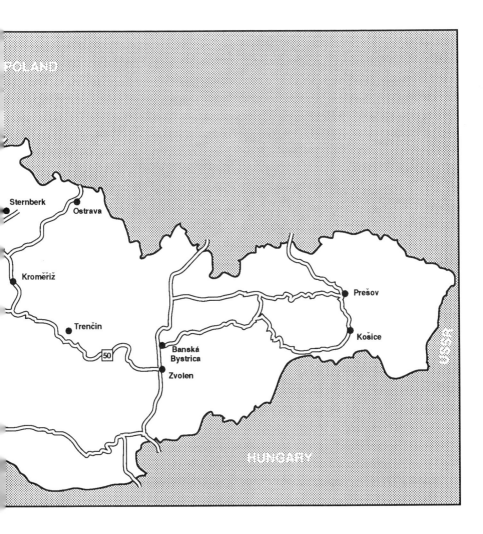

churches seemed, at times, to all but line the roadway. In Šternberk Castle, where no one spoke English, a quick phone call produced a fluent English-speaking guide and his son who took an hour out of their day for a private tour. When it was over, he brushed aside my attempt to pay him for his services. Why, I thought, do these people who have so little insist on giving everything away.

In an off moment, heading out of Kutná Hora, I ran across a carnival that was a photographer's dream. Ladies in babushkas handed over shotguns for the Wild West shooting gallery. There was a swan ride that outdid Disney's flying elephants and a fun house ride with a Transylvanian motif set against the backdrop of a real life medieval castle.

But it was in Banská Bystrica that I found the buoyant enthusiasm of the new regime tempered by the reality of democracy in action. Among the people I met was urban planner Vera Filkova. A person who spent her workday scouring the countryside looking for safe waste disposal sites that will not contaminate the landscape, Vera had good reason to welcome the arrival of the Havel government.

In 1984, her schoolteacher husband had been arrested for the crime of teaching George Orwell's *1984*. At his trial in 1986, Vera had produced a copy of the same novel acquired in the public library in Bratislava. But this did not impress the judge, who sentenced her husband to six months in jail. During this time her son was demoted from the gymnasium to a lesser vocational school. Only through sheer persistence was she able to get her son back into gymnasium and on the college track. After her husband was released, he was denied reemployment in the school system and now works as a private psychologist.

Because his income had dropped, Vera was now the principal support of her family, at a time when her employer, a state planning agency, was slashing its staff. Now she was going to find out firsthand about the challenge of starting her own business. We spoke on the day she moved into her new office, which just happened to be the former headquarters of the local Czech secret police. As workmen carried out the old red stars and other trappings of state socialism, Vera and her colleagues set up shop in the free market. After more than sixteen years of working for the Communist government, she was hanging out her shingle, worrying about bank loans and finding enough business to see her through the first year. "Many people thought the only thing standing between them and great things was the government. It was kind of like a man who had no hands and dreamed of being a sculptor. Miraculously, he awoke one day and found God had given him hands. He went to work and discovered he wasn't a very good sculptor."

"Perhaps a more charitable way to view his dilemma," I suggested over a vast dinner in a baroque dining room, "would be to say that he needed time, like any promising artist, to achieve greatness."

"Ah," Vera told me, "that's just the point. Even with freedom and unlimited time to work at their craft, most people will never be great artists. Now they have a chance to actually realize their own limitations, to realize once and for all that they can no longer blame the state."

Democracy, it seemed, had brought with it a national identity crisis. Assumptions about the new system were being challenged daily. In Prague, friends wanted to know why CNN, the first Western television network to ever appear in Czechoslovakia, was broadcasting censored coverage of the war in the Persian Gulf. "I thought you had a free press," one person told me. Another friend, who had already lost his job in the state price control agency (prices were no longer controlled), was about to lose another part-time job with a dispatch company. "I'm not sure if I can make enough to pay my rent, which is going up very fast," he admitted. And Vera Filkova asked how to cope with democratically elected officials who turned out to be as intractable as their Communist predecessors.

Vera, who lived in one of the prefab Plattenbau high-rises with her husband and son, was fighting to assure that park space was included in the new development. When the new Banská Bystrica mayor refused to vote for open space, Vera was stunned. "It was one of the first big environmental issues he faced, and he was on the wrong side. When I asked why, he announced, 'I'm the mayor and I can do whatever I want.' Can this be democracy?"

Like the rest of Eastern Europe, Czechoslovakia has become a museum of economic and political history. As you travel through this land and see the country making a difficult, at times painful, transition, you are seeing the first culture that has ever tried to switch from a command to a market economy. What that means in human terms has bearing not only on their future but our own. As you meet other Veras during your journey, you will find that liberation is only a beginning, one that poses many questions. Ask a few yourself, and you will probably find that the Czechs are still hopefully looking for the right answers.

ARRIVAL

By Air: CSA, Lufthansa, Delta, British Airways, Air France, and many other airlines have service to Prague. CSA offers nonstop service from New York, and the other carriers reach Czechoslovakia via their European hubs. If you arrive by air, hire a taxi at about 200 crowns ($6.66) for the 20-minute ride into town. Or you can take a CSA (Czechoslovak Airlines) bus that runs every 30 minutes from Ruzyně Airport to the center of town. You will disembark on Hradební Street in front of Vltava terminal station, a 3-minute walk from the Náměstí Republiky subway stop.

By Train: The Main Railway Station (Hlavní nádraží) offers convenient train service to all of Europe. The Czech capital is seven hours from Berlin and four hours from Vienna.

By Car: As a foreigner you need hard currency—dollars, marks, or traveler's checks—to purchase coupons for gas. Sold in $10 units, the coupons are available at the Palace and Intercontinental hotels, banks, and the Kotva department stores. Be sure to specify regular or unleaded coupons, depending on your car. Keep in mind that traveler's checks are not universally accepted. Pragocar, which represents major international rent-a-car firms, has offices at the airport and downtown at Stepanska #42 (tel. 235/2825 or 235/2809). As previously mentioned in the introduction, you will save money by renting your car in Germany or Austria and returning it to that country.

If you're driving from Western Europe, keep in mind that unleaded gasoline (called "natural" here) is often hard to find outside big cities. Buy gas during the day, and do not let your tank slip below half full. Stations may be closed or may have limited hours on holidays. Here is a partial listing of unleaded gas stations in

Czechoslovakia. Additional stations are found on motorways. As mentioned in the introduction, any German ADAC auto club office can provide you with a map of unleaded gas stations in Eastern Europe.

City	Location
Bratislava	Dialničná D-2
	Lamačská Str.
	Petržalka
Brno-Brunn	Kaštanová
	Královopolská
	Okružní
České-Budějovice-Budweis	Dlouhá louka I
Český Krumlov-Krumau	Domoradice
Jihlava-Iglau	Břenská Str.
Karlovry-Vary-Karlsbad	Drahovice I
Kosice	Moldavska cesta
Kutná Hora-Kuttenberg	(Inquire at Čedok)
Olomouc	Břenská A
	Prazska A
Pardubiče	Chrudimska Str.
Pilsen	Rokycanska I
Prague	Holešovice, Argentinská
	Petřiny, Mackova
	Malá Chuchle
	Ceskebredská
Tábor	Klokoty
Telč	(Inquire at Čedok)
Teplice	Richtg. Prag, Prosetice
Třeboň	Třeboň
Zvolen	Rakos

MONEY

After you arrive, you will want to buy some crowns. For a quick rough conversion from crowns to U.S. dollars, multiply the crown amount by 3.3 and then move the decimal point two places to the left. For example, 30 crowns equals about $1.00.

TELEPHONE

As with all calls from the United States, you must first dial 011 for international long distance, then 42 for the country code. The city code for Prague is 2. Thus, a call to the number 345-8942 in Prague from the United States should be dialed 011-42-2-345-8942. From Czechoslovakia, use USA Direct to phone home. The access number is 042-0010. Within Czechoslovakia, you must first dial 0 before the area code and number for a long distance call to another part of the country. Area codes relevant to cities in this book are České Budějovice (38), Telč (96), Tábor (361), Olomouc (68), Kroměříž (634), Kutná Hora (327), Pardubiče (40), and Trenčín (831).

Prague

Prague looks like it was built for a fairy tale. It exemplifies many of the reasons Eastern Europe has become a hot ticket among discerning travelers. Unlike much of urban Western Europe, it has been spared the blight of postmodernist commercial construction. Instead of glass curtain wall high-rises, you will see the Europe of the imagination. Miraculously spared devastation during World War II, this city endures as a marvelous blend of baroque, Romanesque, and Gothic architecture on the Vltava River. Pařižská Street, one of the handsomest promenades on the continent, Old Town Square with its fanciful clock, the Jewish Museum, and Hradčany Castle, the subject of Franz Kafka's novel *The Castle*, are just a few of Prague's noteworthy attractions.

An architectural shrine, this city is also a pedestrian's dream with such spots as the Charles Bridge, the Malá Strana District, and Wenceslas Square, the latter the scene of mass demonstrations that led to the recent fall of the Communist regime. The medieval core

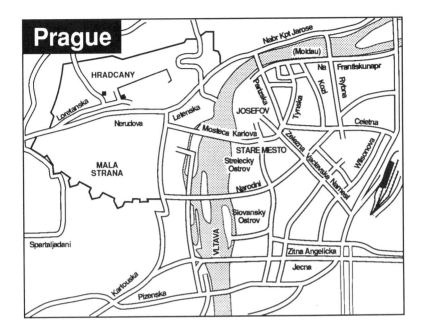

of the city is crowned by Prague Castle and St. Vitus Cathedral. An evening view of these illuminated landmarks from the Charles Bridge is one of the most memorable sights in all Europe. Visiting Prague today is a little like being part of a celebration of the Fourth of July, Thanksgiving, and Christmas rolled into one. The atmosphere is electric. Emerging from more than forty years of Communist domination, the Czechs herald their newfound liberty every day. At last they can buy independent newspapers where the truth extends beyond the sports section.

Reborn Prague can be crowded during the peak summer months, but it is a delight to visit at any time of year. Spring and fall are highly recommended. Czechoslovakia, the only country in the world run by a playwright, is in the midst of a difficult political and economic transformation. You'll surely learn about it firsthand as you explore the streets of Prague, a city in control of its own destiny for the first time in half a century.

GETTING AROUND

For general information, it is a good idea to head directly to the government-run Čedok tourist office at Na příkopě #18 (tel. 212/7111) for maps, current events schedules, and helpful brochures. Here you will be able to pick up information on the efficient bus and subway network that serves the city. The new **American Hospitality Center** at Malé náměstí 14, next to the Old Town Square, can also help orient you, change money, and serve as a message center. Also here is **Prague Suites**, a booking service. Call 236/7486. Both Čedok at its Bílkova #6 office (tel. 231/6619) and **Prague Information Service** at Panská #4 (tel. 224/311) provide tourist services such as city tours with English-speaking guides.

There are three important railway stations in Prague, and they are all situated on metro stops. The Main Railway Station (Hlavní nádraží) is placed on Line C, stop Hlavni nádraží; Prague-Holešovice Station (Nádraží Holešovice), Line C; and Masaryk Railway Station (náměstí Republiky), Line B. Before you enter the subway, buy a ticket from the machines at the entrance. Maps of the subway are posted in the stations and inside the trains. Recorded announcements en route identify the stops. The subway runs from 5:00 a.m. to midnight.

Taxis can be found outside hotels, railway stations, and museums. Radio taxis can be booked by tel. 203/941 or 202/951. Or you can phone Taxi Reax, tel. 549/9571. Cabs are inexpensive, but insist that the driver use the meter or quote a fare before departing.

LODGING

If you want first-class accommodations, particularly in the summer months, advance reservations are mandatory. Although Prague is a moderately priced city by European standards, the good hotels here are no great bargain. And keep in mind that as these establishments convert to private ownership in 1991, prices are expected to increase. Expect to pay a premium in high season.

The art nouveau **Palace Hotel** at Panská #12 is located in the heart of Prague, just two minutes from Wenceslas Square (tel. 236/0008; fax 235/9373) runs $230 to $350. For remarkable views of the Old Town houses and Týnský church at Old Town Square, book a room at the **Ungelt Hotel**, Štupartská #1 (tel. 232/0470).

Old Town Square, Prague, Czechoslovakia

They run $170 to $210. Located in a modern building on Kongresová #1, two subway stops from the center of town, the **Forum Hotel** runs $164 to $290 (tel. 410/111). The neo-Gothic **Paříž Hotel**, five minutes from Old Town Square at U Obecního domu #1 (tel. 238/0820), is famous for its art nouveau interior. It is also a national cultural monument. Rooms run $88 to $131. On Wenceslas Square, the art nouveau **Europa Hotel** enjoys an ideal location for people watching. It's at Václavske náměstí #25 (tel. 263/7469) and rooms run 1,837 to 2,652 crowns ($73 to $106). In the Malá Strana, **U Tří Pštrosů**, Dražického #12, enjoys one of the most romantic locations in town at the end of the Charles Bridge. Built in 1597, this nicely restored building offers rooms from 1,620 to 5,000 crowns ($65 to $200). Tel. 536/007. There is also a restaurant and wine bar.

Prague has a number of moderately priced hotels. You can expect shared bath facilities in many of these establishments. All of those mentioned below are heavily booked and have restaurants of their own. Do not expect luxury here. In Nové Město close to Karlova Square, the **Moráň Hotel** at Na Moráni #15 (tel. 294/251) is a ten-minute walk from the city center. Rooms run 635 to 735

Old Town Hall Clock Tower, Prague, Czechoslovakia

crowns ($25 to $29). The **Kriváň** at I.P. Pavolva #5, also in Nové Město (tel. 293/341), runs 550 to 700 crowns ($13 to $21). The **Balkán** at #28 Svornosti (tel. 540/777) in the Smíchov district near the Vltava runs 550 to 700 crowns ($18 to $23). The **Ostaš Hotel**, located at Orebitska #8 (tel. 272/860) in the Žižkov district about ten minutes from the center, offers rooms for 800 to 1,500 crowns ($27 to $50) including a half pension. The **Juventus** in the Vinohrady district at Blanická #10 (tel. 255/151) is also just ten minutes by metro from the center. Rooms run 350 to 612 crowns ($12 to $20).

Four inexpensive student hostels are also available in Prague. For booking information, contact Čedok at Panská #5 (tel. 225/657 or 227/004). Čedok can also recommend a number of camping facilities in the Prague area. Most open in May and close in September or October.

If you want to meet the people of Prague and save money, consider a homestay. Čedok's booking office at Panská #5 can recommend inexpensive bed-and-breakfast facilities. If you do not mind sharing a bath, this is an excellent way to get acquainted with the Czechs. Some of your most memorable moments in Prague will be spent visiting with your hosts. It is a good idea to bring along a small gift. Expect to pay $10 to $30 a night.

Several travel agencies also arrange private accommodations. **Pragotour** at U Prašné brány #1090 (tel. 231/7281) and **AVE** at the Praha-Holešovice railway station office also have listings. The AVE main office is at Wilsonova #80 (tel. 236/2560). Another possibility is **ARTOUR**, Ondráček, Karolíny Světlé #9 (tel. 235/8389; fax 235/8389). Among the many hosts who book their own rooms is Miroslav Jirsak. Tel. 738/709. He frequently takes guests staying at his apartment on a delightful walking tour of the Prague castle and other local highlights.

A more expensive alternative is **Prague Suites**, which books 260 centrally located, unhosted apartments. Available for stays of three nights or longer, these apartments also have concierge service and minivan pickup from the airport and rail station. Units run $100 a night (per group, not per person) and up. Locations include Old Town Square and the Charles Bridge. This company can also recommend less expensive homestays in hosted apartments if you visit their office in Prague on Male náměstí near Old Town Square. For more information, call 267/770. Their fax number is 269/738.

FOOD

Prague restaurants are great fun. And if your approach is positive and flexible, you will find them one of the best parts of your stay. Prague restaurants come in four price categories; the most expensive demand reservations. Most second price category restaurants serve wine but not beer, which explains why they are known as winehouses. For a beer, you will want to go to a third or fourth category restaurant or a local pub. Keep in mind that the prices here are going up as private enterprise completes the takeover of restaurants from the state.

Parnas at Smetanovo Nábřeží #2 (tel. 265/017) has a beautiful view of Hradčany Castle. You will be entertained by a concert pianist in the paneled dining room. This first price category winehouse is open daily from 7:00 p.m. to 1:00 a.m., except during the summer, when it's closed on Sunday. Reservations are mandatory. For a snack or coffee, visit the **Slavia** café next to Parnas opposite the National Theatre.

In the second price category, you can try homemade sausages known as Strapečky at **Dům Slovenské Kultury**, Purkyňova #4 (tel. 291/996). During the summer months, enjoy dining out on the terrace. There is also a basement wine room. It's open daily except Sunday from 4:00 p.m. to 2:00 a.m. **Klášterní Vinárna** at Národní #8 (tel. 290/596) offers a wide-ranging menu ranging from chateaubriand to "Prelate's" pancakes. A monastery winehouse offers an impressive selection. Open from 11:00 a.m. to 1:00 a.m. Reservations are mandatory. **U Cervenehó Kola** at Anežská #2/4 (tel. 231/8941) offers both Czech and international cuisine. It is open daily from 10:00 a.m. to 10:00 p.m. For Bohemian and international dishes, try **Valdštejnská hospoda** at Tomášká #16 (tel. 536/195). It is open daily from 11:00 a.m. to 3:00 p.m. and 6:00 p.m. to 11:00 p.m. Reservations are required. Czech beer is great. A good place to try it on tap is **U Modré Štiky**, Karlova #20 (tel. 263/065). This fish house is open daily from 9:00 a.m. to 11:00 p.m. For old-style Czech cuisine, try **U Pinkasů** at Jungmannovo náměstí #14 (tel. 261/804). It is open from 7:00 a.m. to 3:00 p.m. and 4:00 p.m. to midnight.

Charles Bridge, Prague, Czechoslovakia

NIGHTLIFE

For concert tickets, try the box office at **Smetana Hall**, Municipal House, #5 náměstí Republiky. Tel. 232/5858. Concerts begin at 7:30 p.m. Or head to **Prague Culture Palace**, Ul. 5. Května 65 (tel. 417/2711). The best of Mozart/Opera Mozart is at Smetana Museum on Novotného lávka. **Prague Opera Furore** in Malostranská Beseda is at Malostranské náměstí. For jazz, try **Press Jazz Club**, Pařížská #9, or **Supraclub** at Opletova #5.

SIGHTSEEING

Prague Castle

The ideal place to begin a Prague visit is the seat of power, Hradčany Castle. This citadel, brilliantly lit at night, has been the heart of Czech politics for more than 1,000 years. A tour of the castle complex, which is flanked by palaces, churches, monasteries and galleries, can easily occupy an entire day. While at the castle, you can see beautiful religious objects in the **Cathedral Treasury** and the art collection of Holy Roman Emperor Rudolf II in the **Castle Gallery**.

To reach the castle complex, take tram #22 from the city center to Památník Písemnictví station. Then walk through Pohořelec Square to the **Strahov Monastery** and the **Museum of National Literature**. The museum is open daily except Monday from 9:00 a.m. to 5:00 p.m. The church and monastery gardens here offer a grand view of the Czech capital. You will want to explore the frescoed Theological and Philosophical halls before visiting the Strahov Library, famous for its illuminated manuscripts that include the ninth- and tenth-century Strahov Gospels.

Return to Pohořelec Square and walk down toward the castle. En route, visit the **Loretto Church** and the adjacent **Černín Palace** that currently serves as the Ministry of Foreign Affairs. Continue to Hradčanské náměstí. On the left side of the **Archbishop's Palace**, you will see a small alley leading to the **Šternberk Palace**. This baroque monument is famous for its European art galleries that include an entire Picasso room. On the south side of Hradčanské náměstí is the **Schwarzenberg Palace**, home of the **Museum of Military History**. A gem of the Prague Renaissance, this collection showcases battle memorabilia from across the continent.

Continue east to St. Vitus Cathedral where twenty-one chapels offer a panoramic view of European architecture, art, and religious

Kafka's house, Golden Lane, Prague, Czechoslovakia

tradition. Begun in the fourteenth century, the cathedral complex was no rush job. The six-century project was finally completed in 1929. Among the highlights are the 30-foot-high rose window, the Romanesque rotunda of St. Wenceslas Chapel, and the frescoed ceilings of the Chapel of the Holy Rood. In the Crown Chamber, you will see the coronation jewels of the Bohemian kings and a fourteenth-century gold crown.

The individual buildings in the castle area are open daily except Monday in summer from 9:00 a.m. to 5:00 p.m. and in winter from 9:00 a.m. to 4:00 p.m. At Vikářská #37, there is an Information Center that also provides guide services. **Golden Lane**, also known as Goldmaker's Alley, is found behind St. George's monastery. Ask any of the castle guides for directions to this street with its tiny pastel-colored houses. Of special interest is #22, where Franz Kafka lived and wrote. On this street, alchemists tried and failed to discover how to make gold for Rudolf II.

Malostranské Square and the Charles Bridge

After completing your Prague Castle visit, return to Hradčanské Square. Walk west on Loretánská Street until you reach Radnické schody, which loops back east to Nerudova. Continue east on Nerudova Street to the palaces of Malostranské Square, the heart of Lesser Town or Little Quarter Town. With its small shops, pubs, churches, palaces, and narrow cobblestone streets, this is one of the most inviting neighborhoods in Eastern Europe. Here in the heart of the Malá Strana District, you will want to visit St. Nicholas Church and relax at the Malostranské Café.

From Malostranské Square, take Mostecká Street east toward the river to Lázeňská Street. Turn right and head south to Maltezske Square. Continue east toward the river until you reach Velkopřevorské Square. On your right is the Lennon Wall, where Czechs still gather to honor the Beatle's memory. Next cross the footbridge over the Čertovka Stream. Continue north on Hroznová Street to Kampa Square. At the north end of Kampá are stairs leading to the **Charles Bridge**. Or, if you prefer, walk beneath the Charles Bridge to U Lužického semináře Street and Dražického Square. From here, you will want to head east across the Charles Bridge.

View from Charles Bridge of Kampa Street, Prague, Czechoslovakia

This Gothic bridge, adorned by thirty baroque statues, is one of the most popular spots in Prague. You can buy a fine painting here from one of the street artists, photograph the birds that sail into view on cue, or book a dinner reservation at U Tří Pštrosù (tel. 536/151), perfectly situated at the west end. On the north end is Na Kampě, a romantic lane that invites evening exploration. The statues that date back to the seventeenth century immortalize saints, knights, and Christ. No matter how short your stay, do not miss this bridge, one of the highlights of any visit to Eastern Europe.

Old Town Square and Josefov

Easily reached by taking Karlova Street east from the Charles Bridge, Old Town Square is the site of the Old Town Hall, distinguished by its clock tower richly appointed with zodiac signs. Every hour, a skeletal figure of death turns an hourglass upside down and the twelve apostles march out of the timepiece to musical accompaniment. Joining the fun are other figures representing Vanity and Greed. Open-air restaurants make the square a delight. In 1948, the Communists celebrated their takeover of the country here. In winter 1989, Václav Havel declared the liberation of his country from the same location. Old Town Hall, built in the fourteenth century, was partially destroyed during World War II, but most of the building endures as a Gothic monument with a fine baroque interior. Nearby are Romanesque **Kinský Palace** and **Týn Church** with its twin black towers. **Pařížská Street**, the finest street in Prague, begins on the northwest side of the square. With its classic art nouveau buildings and beautiful shops, this is the perfect route north into **Josefov**, the old Jewish Quarter.

One of the happiest results of Prague's liberation is the restoration of the city's Jewish community. Hitler's storm troopers exterminated more than 90 percent of Czechoslovakia's roughly 100,000 Jews in concentration camps. Many were taken from this historic area. Originally the Prague ghetto, this is the home of one of the continent's oldest Jewish communities. The sixteenth-century Jewish Town Hall has been the heart of Josefov for more than four centuries. Liberated from their ghetto by Hapsburg Emperor Joseph II at the end of the nineteenth century, the Jews continued to worship at their six local synagogues. But when the Germans rolled into

Czechoslovakia, the synagogues were all closed. Beautiful textiles and silver works, Hebrew manuscripts, paintings, and religious artifacts were collected from the nation's synagogues during World War II by eminent Jewish curators. Selected by Hitler's lieutenants, these curators were told to create a "museum of Jewish culture" that would, after the "inevitable" Nazi victory, become a showcase of an "extinct culture." As Hitler's storm troopers decimated the Jewish people of Czechoslovakia, these experts were assigned to comb through abandoned synagogues and ship the very best treasures back to Prague.

In the capital city, the temples became warehouses for this collection that would be exhibited as soon as the war ended. When the job was finished, the curators were rewarded for their hard work by being sent to the concentration camps, where they perished. After the war, the Prague government decided to complete the **State Jewish Museum**, not as a memorial but as a living testament to this persecuted people.

This Jewish Museum, located on Pařížská Street in the heart of Josefov, is composed of six temples now serving as exhibit space. The **Old New Synagogue**, Europe's oldest synagogue is distinguished by its Torah display. The **High Synagogue** contains one of Europe's finest examples of sacred Jewish textiles. Near this Gothic classic is the baroque **Cells Synagogue**, which has an exceptional collection of Hebrew books and manuscripts. The neo-Gothic **Maisel Synagogue** is famous for its handsome exhibit of silver treasures. At the **Pinkas Synagogue**, you will find inscriptions memorializing more than 77,000 Czech Jews who perished in the Holocaust.

Located adjacent to the Jewish Museum is the **Jewish Cemetery**, a fifteenth-century burial ground that served the community until the late eighteenth century. Because space was limited, early graves were covered with dirt to make space for new tombs. Because the cemetery ground slumped unevenly, the landscape is jagged, with tombstones listing at all angles. A monument to the courage and dedication of the Prague Jewish community, this inspiring memorial invites exploration. Happily, with the support of the new democratic government, they are now rebuilding their proud tradition.

Mikuláš Church, Mala Strana District, Prague, Czechoslovakia

From Josefov, take Bílkova Street east to Dušní Street and the **Church of Saint Duch**. This fourteenth-century landmark was partially rebuilt in the baroque style in 1689. Turn right to U Milosrdných Street, and one of the oldest early Gothic monuments of Czech Christianity—the **Convent of the Blessed Agnes**. Inside are classic nineteenth-century Czech paintings. Follow Anežská Street to Hastelské Square. On the southeast side of the square, pick up Rybna Street and turn right to Masná Street; then go left to M. Štupartská Street. Here you will see the baroque **Church of Saint Jakub**. Then take Jakubska Street to the **Powder Tower**. Built in the fifteenth century, this fortification served as a gunpowder store-room. Located adjacent to the royal home, the tower was done over with a neo-Gothic roof during the late nineteenth century. Today it is a landmark on the Royal Way, the coronation route that leads up from Old Town Square and Karlova over the Charles Bridge and up to the castle. Continue west on Celetná Street to Staroměstské Square, and from there, turn left on Železná Street to the **Stavouské Theater** where Mozart's *Don Giovanni* premiered in 1787.

Wenceslas Square/Na Příkopě/Národní

Center of the 1989 Prague revolution, **Wenceslas Square** is the heart of modern Prague. When you visit you will likely see people from all walks of life putting out flowers and candles in memory of Jan Palach, the young patriot who immolated himself here in 1968. At the top of the square directly behind the statue of St. Wenceslas, Bohemia's patron saint, is the **National Museum**. To the right are the Federal Assembly and the Smetana Theater. This square, with grand hotels like the Europa, invites leisurely exploration.

At the end of the square the first main intersection leads right into **Na Příkopě**, a pedestrian zone in the city's main shopping area. Here you will find the Čedok office, theaters, bookstores, department stores, and tourist offices. Turn left and you will be on Národní Street, which will take you to the **National Theater** overlooking the Vltava. During the summer months, you can walk across the bridge to **Slavonic Island** (Slovanský Ostrov) or enjoy a steamboat cruise. Another possibility is a trip on tram #17 to Vyšehrad, once the site of Přemyslids Castle. Here you will find the National Cemetery where many of the nation's best-known scientists, artists, and political leaders are buried.

Konopiště Castle and Karlštejn Castle

An easy one-hour train journey from Prague's main railway station (tel. 264/930), Konopiště is just 2 kilometers from the Benešov station. The castle's last owner was the successor to the Austrian-Hungarian throne, Franz Ferdinand d'Este. Set in an English-style park with a fine rose garden, the castle features a vast weapons collection and an exhibit on St. George. The castle is an impressive memorial to the archduke. He and his wife were assassinated in Sarajevo—the shots that triggered World War I. Open April through October, daily except Mondays, from 9:00 a.m. to 4:00 p.m. (5:00 p.m. in peak summer season). Tel. 030/12460.

Another possibility is Karlštejn Castle, reached by a 40-minute train ride from Smíchovske nádraží railway station. This Gothic castle perched atop a rocky hill is a 20-minute walk from the rail station. The castle, which overlooks the valley of the Berounka, was built in the fourteenth century by the Emperor Charles IV. The frescoed Church of Our Lady is an art museum in itself.

Specialized Shops

Prague's wonderful artisans and artists make it an ideal place to look for souvenirs. Why not visit a few to see some of the best work, sold at very reasonable prices. From ceramics to handmade dolls, good deals abound.

Jewelry: Bijoux de Bohème, Staroměstské #6 (tel. 231/7771). Other locations include Na příkopě #12, Václavské náměstí #53, and Národní #25.

Glass and Porcelain: Bohemia/Moser, Na přikopé #12, Praha 1. Other locations include Malé náměstí #6, Václavské #3, Pařížská #2, and Celetná #26.

Artistic Products: Česka jizba, Karlova #12 (tel. 265/773), Krasna Jizba, Národní #36 (tel. 236/6535), Slovenská jizba, Václavské náměstí 40 (tel. 235/2967), and UVA, Na příkopě #25 (tel. 262/879).

Musical Instruments: P-1, Jungmannovo náměstí # 17 (tel. 236/1376). Another branch is located at Michalská #3 (tel. 224/496).

Souvenirs: P-1 at Václavské náměstí #47. Branches are located at Staroměstské náměstí #6, Malé náměstí #10, and Na Mustku #81.

Antique Goods: P-1 antique stores are located at Mikulandská #7, Národní #22, Celetná #31, Václavské #60, Nerudova #46, Karlova #2, and Mostecká #22.

Department Stores: Kotva, náměstí Republiky #8, Máj, Národní #26, Družba, Václavské náměstí #21, and Bílá Labuť, Na poříčí #23.

Southern Bohemia and Moravia

J ust two hours from Prague, southern Bohemia and Moravia should be your first choice for a look at rural Czechoslovakia. If your time is limited, you could drive down to Telč and Český Krumlov for a day and still make it back to Prague that evening. But we recommend a more leisurely trip of two or three days. Using České Budějovice as your hub, you can visit your choice of half a dozen castle towns, each a gem and each a step back in time. Except for an occasional billboard looking for an advertiser ("This is a billboard, it sells your products"), you will find a region that has been spared most of the commercialism that is beginning to alter the face of the big Eastern European cities. In fact, South Bohemia is a place the Czechs themselves turn to when they want to remind themselves of the good old days.

What can you expect in this region? Perhaps the finest small town square in Eastern Europe. Certainly one of the region's most majestic castles. Augustinian monasteries, ale houses, and Renaissance fountains, semicircular bastions, châteaus that attract tourists from France, Gothic wall paintings, frescoed palaces that attract tourists from Italy, and, of course, beautiful countryside. No matter how long you spend in South Bohemia you will wish you could stay longer.

GETTING THERE

Located 90 miles south of Prague, České Budějovice is three hours by train or car. The Čedok office at #38 náměstí Premysla Otakara is a good place to get up-to-date information on this region. Tel. 38/35751.

LODGING

In České Budějovice, the **Hotel Zvon**, náměstí Premysla Otakara #2, offers rooms at about 1,000 crowns ($33). Tel. 383/5361. (Remember to add a 0 in front of the area code if you are calling long distance within Czechoslovakia.) **Hotel Grand** at Nádrazní #27

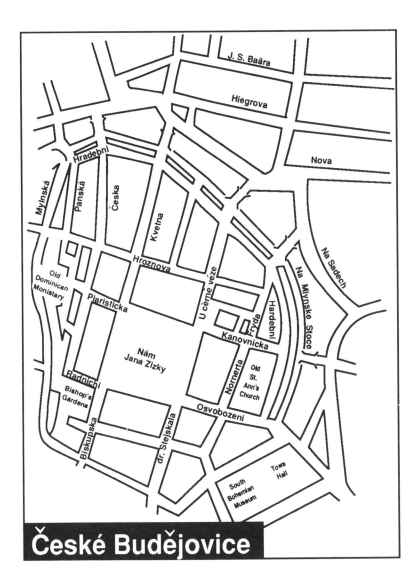

Český Budějovice

offers rooms that start around 900 crowns ($30). Tel. 383/6591. Accommodations in private apartments and homes can be arranged through Čedok at Svornosti náměstí #4. Tel. 383/2279. This office can also provide information on camping and hostels in the area.

Třeboň, southern Bohemia

If you prefer to stay in Telč, a room at **Hotel Černy Orel** on the famous square at #7 Zachariase Hradče runs 350 crowns (about $12). Tel. 96/2221. In Český Krumlov, the **Hotel Krumlov** at #14 Svornosti náměstí runs about 350 crowns (about $12). Tel. 337/2255.

FOOD

In České Budějovice, **Hotel Gomel**, #14 Míru třida, has two restaurants, including the **Rybářská**, which specializes in fish. Tel. 28949. In Telč, try the restaurants at the Hotel Černy Orel. In Český Krumlov, we recommend the restaurant at the **Hotel Krumlov**.

SIGHTSEEING

Thanks to its central location, České Budějovice, a town of 92,000, is the best gateway to South Bohemia. You will find it easy to take convenient day trips to the principal historic towns and castles in this region that has over 5,000 recognized historical monuments. Of course, České Budějovice, founded in 1265, is a major destination in its own right. The historic town, created to strengthen royal power against incursions by feudal lords, is a classic example of the medieval village. Among the city's highlights are the monastery garden, the Gothic-Renaissance armory, the baroque Samson's Fountain, and the Black Tower, which served as watchtower and belfry for the Church of Saint Nicholas.

České Budějovice is the home of Europe's pioneer horse-drawn railway, which began service in 1832. The city is also known for its Budweis beer, produced here for nearly a century (sorry, no Clydesdales here). After exploring the city, you will want to head out to visit some of South Bohemia's smaller towns such as Telč, Třeboň and Český Krumlov. You can reach them by rental car, bus, or a Čedok-arranged tour. It is also possible to hire a local taxi driver. Each of these destinations is within an hour of České Budějovice. If you have the time, we urge you to see all three.

Telč

Famous for its town square, this Moravian village makes you feel like you've stepped inside a fairy tale. Located 50 miles northeast of České Budějovice (77 miles southeast of Prague) at the convergence

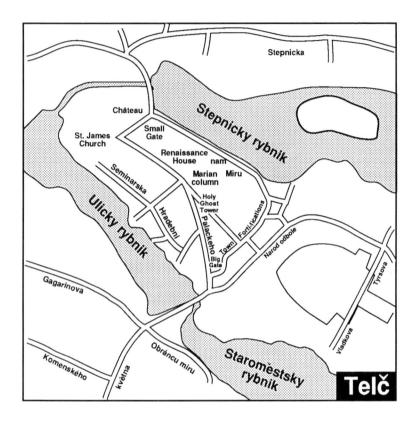

of trade routes that connected Austria, Moravia, and Bohemia, Telč
dates back to the eleventh century. The town you see, built around
a trapezoid-shaped square, dates back to the fourteenth century. It
was Zacharias of Hradec, the squire of Telč, and his wife, Catherine
of Valdstejn, who turned Telč into a showplace beginning in 1553.
They hired Italian artisans and stucco workers to transform the
medieval bastion into a grand and glorious Renaissance **castle**. The
finest furniture, silver, gold-plated chairs, and goblets were used to
ornament the great banquet hall of this castle paid for by the profits
of his gold and silver mines. Construction continued for more than
thirty years with the addition of a sepulchral chapel, garden arcades,
and, of course, a moat.

The castle alone is enough to justify a visit to Telč. As you walk through this palace, you will see the hunting weapons of several lords of the manor, baroque furniture added in the seventeenth century, Meissen porcelain, an eighteenth-century clock, and paintings by the Austrian masters. After visiting here, you will want to continue out to the famous square with its arcaded Renaissance and Gothic homes. Many of these buildings are painted in bright pastels, and a number have been turned into shops and restaurants. Two gates have been preserved here, as has the thirteenth-century **Church of the Holy Ghost** with its Romanesque steeple. If you only have time to visit one South Bohemian village, let this be it.

Třeboň

Located 15 miles east of České Budějovice (84 miles southeast of Prague), Třeboň was the domain of the Rožmberk family, which founded the **Augustine Monastery** here in 1367. This noble family, and the Schwarzenbergs who succeeded them in 1660, made Třeboň one of the most enchanting towns in Bohemia.

Enter via the Budejovicka gate and turn into the famed monastery. Among its highlights is the frescoed fourteenth-century

South Bohemia, Czechoslovakia

monastery cloister. During the baroque era, Gothic paintings by the famed masters of Třeboň were hung in churches around town. You can still see some of them in the old Augustinian monastery church. Also worth a visit is the **Church of St. Giles**, famous for its restored Gothic frescoes.

Like Telč, Třeboň is known for its town square with pastel-colored Renaissance and baroque buildings. Perhaps the best-known structure is the corner building, U Bílého koníčka. On the south side you will find a one-story town hall built in 1566. The stone fountain on the square was built in 1569, and the Plague Column was added in the eighteenth century.

Dominating the city's historic core is **Třeboň Castle**, notable for its three-story arcade and Renaissance stairway in the inner courtyard. To reach the castle garden walk through Lipova Park. Be sure to stroll down Brezanova Ulice for a look at its arcades and gabled homes. Be sure not to miss the pseudo-Gothic **Schwarzenberg Tomb**, which was built in the nineteenth century. Also worth a visit is the cemetery of the **Church of St. Aegidus**, which includes an altar portrait of William of Rožmberk and his two wives.

Třeboň is also famous for its fish ponds rimmed by towering oaks. Aquaculture in this region began in the mid-fifteenth century. It was Stepan Netolicky who convinced local estate owners to create these ponds with the help of the **Golden Canal** that drained surplus water from the Luznice River. This 27-mile canal remains the hub of a pond system still used to breed carp. **Svět Pond**, just beyond the town walls, is popular for swimming in the warm months. The annual fishing out of the **Rožmberk Pond**, 3.6 miles north of town, is a major fall event. Adjacent to Rožmberk is a string of popular lakes including **Velký and Malý Tisý**, two major Czech bird sanctuaries.

Český Krumlov

A splendid medieval town on the banks of the Vltava, Český Krumlov has more than 300 historic buildings. Located at the base of the Smava mountains, the town is best known for its monumental castle begun by the lords of Krumlov. The town was founded by the Vítovci family in the early thirteenth century. Their successors, the Rožmberks, governed their vast domain from a seat here from the

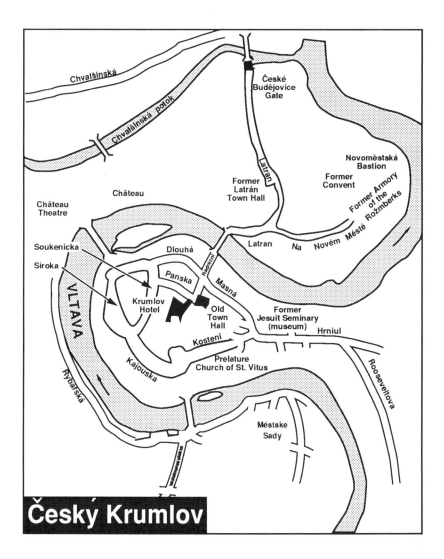

Český Krumlov

fourteenth to the seventeenth century. Determined to compete with
Prague, the Rožmberks spared no expense as they brought in Italian architects and masons to add a Renaissance flavor to this Gothic
town and castle. They were followed by the Eggenbergs who built
a castle garden and theater and the Schwarzenbergs who added
baroque monuments in the eighteenth and nineteenth centuries.

Popular with nineteenth-century painters, Český Krumlov attracts eager visitors from all over Europe. UNESCO has called it one of Europe's most historically important attractions. The leading attraction is the **Krumlov Castle**, the largest feudal residence in the country after the Prague Castle. The castle has Gothic, Renaissance, and baroque components and a round tower and is a national landmark. One of the best rooms is the frescoed Masquerade Hall. In the garden, you will find a fountain adorned with statues, the Bellarie summerhouse, and a historic seventeenth-century theater.

Theater festivals are held annually in Český Krumlov. But do not worry if you miss the drama here. Simply walking through the town is an event. During your visit, explore the city's medieval core, making your way past fourteenth-century homes, landmarks like the fifteenth-century **Church of St. Vitus**, and the sixteenth-century burgrave's house. Be sure not to miss the historic buildings of the Latran district on the left bank of the Vltava. There's also a notable town hall here. Also, visit the town museum at #152 Horní ulice. It's open Tuesday and Thursday through Saturday from 9:00 a.m. to noon and 12:30 to 4:00 p.m., Wednesday 9:00 a.m. to noon and 12:30 to 6:00 p.m. On Sundays, hours are 9:00 a.m. to noon. Tel. 337/2049.

About 4 miles northeast of Český Krumlov is **Zlatá Koruna**, the thirteenth-century Cistercian monastery famous for its Gothic church.

Moravia and Slovakia

For a small country, Czechoslovakia has a seemingly inexhaustible fund of historic towns, castles, museums, monuments, and rural retreats. Some of the area's great cities are easily accessible from Prague in a convenient loop. If you are driving to or from our recommended Hungarian great cities, this is an easy way to make your trip a special one. Many of these cities are also accessible by train or a Čedok guided tour. No matter how you travel, expect to see the heart of the country in a relaxed and informal manner. While it is true that you will not find the kind of five-star accommodations available in Prague, there are convenient hotels as well as homestays that can be arranged through local Čedok offices. In all these towns, expect to spend each day strolling through pedestrian-oriented town squares and visiting castles and cathedrals, small museums, and, of course, fine parks that will add to your enjoyment. Many Czech visitors find these smaller towns the most memorable part of their journey. Perhaps you will, too.

LODGING

In Kutná Hora, try the **Hotel Medinek**, Palackého náměstí, where rooms run about 720 crowns ($24). Tel. 327/2741. Čedok at Palackého náměstí #157 can also arrange homestays. Tel. 327/3510.

In Olomouc, the **Palác International Hotel** at #1 Máje 27 offers rooms in the 900 crown range ($30). Tel. 682/4096. You can also book a room through Čedok at Horní náměstí #2. Tel. 682/8831.

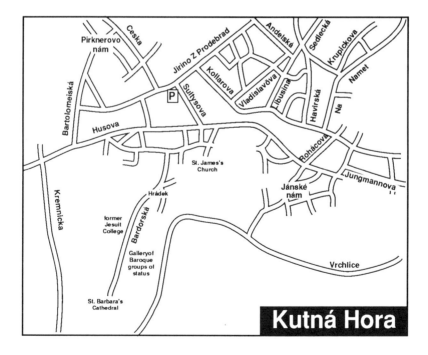

Pirknerovo nám

Ceska

Jirino Z Prodebrad

Andelska

Sedlecka

Krupickova

Bartolomeiská

Kollarova

Vladislavova

Libusina

Havirská

Namet

Na

Husova

P

Suhysova

Rohácova

St. James's Church

Jungmannova

Jánské nám

Kremnicka

Hrádek

former Jesuit College

Bardorská

Galleryof Baroque groups of status

Vrchlice

St. Barbara's Cathedral

Kutná Hora

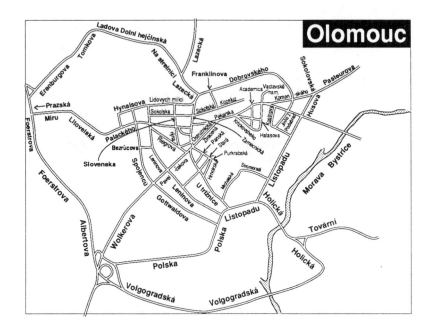

Prostějov's **Hotel Avion**, náměstí Eduarda Husserla #15, runs about 250 crowns ($8.50). Tel. 508/4561. Also try the **Grandhotel**, Palackého #3, with rooms in the same price range. Tel. 508/4257. The **Čedok** office is at Netusilova #5. Tel. 508/5974. In Kroměříž you can stay at **Hotel Hana** on Velké náměstí. It has rooms starting at 250 crowns ($8.50). Tel. 634/22804. **Čedok** is located at Tovačovského #3161. Tel. 634/21462.

Hotel Laugaricio in Trenčín on Vajanskeho náměstí has rooms beginning at 300 crowns ($10). Tel. 831/37841. **Čedok** at Mierové náměstí #34 can arrange homestays. Tel. 831/35107.

FOOD

In Kutná Hora, we recommend **U Anděla**, on Václavské náměstí. Tel. 327/2040. In Kroměříž, try **Hotel Hana** on Velké náměstí. Tel. 327/21715. Olomouc's **Hanacka** restaurant is a good bet. Tel. 68/26971. Prostějov's **Hotel Avion** is located at Eduarda Husserla #15. Tel. 508/4565. In Trenčín, dine at **Tatra**, SNP #2. Tel. 831/34331.

Castle built on the site of a Roman fortress, Trenčín, Czechoslovakia

Town Square, Telč, Czechoslovakia

SIGHTSEEING

Begin exploring this region by heading east 40 miles from Prague to Kutná Hora. This town is famous for its medieval and baroque homes, **Royal Palace**, and **Cathedral of St. Barbara**. Also of special interest is the **Italian Court**, a Gothic classic famous for its silver coin collection. During your visit be sure to visit the **Archdeacon's House**, a Renaissance building with a red marble portal, and the **Stone Fountain** on Rejskovo náměstí. In Sedlec, just a mile from the center of Kutná Hora, is the wonderful baroque **Church of Our Lady**.

Continue east about two hours to the central Moravian town of Olomouc. Located on the Morava River, this town is famous for its Romanesque **castle**, a national monument. The historic district has a beautiful town hall with a Renaissance loggia and a fifteenth-century astronomical clock. **St. Wenceslas's Cathedral**, the **Church of Our Lady of the Snows**, and the **Church of St. Maurice** are all

Moravia, Czechoslovakia

worth a visit. Also take the short drive (about 20 minutes) north to Šternberk and the **Šternberk Castle**. If you are lucky, the office may be able to arrange an English-speaking guide. Be sure to ask. This is one of the finest small castles in the country, blessed with a terrific clock museum, one of the best in Europe. From sundials to elegant handpainted dials from the Middle Ages, this is a one-of-a-kind collection. Do not miss it.

Convenient to Olomouc are Prostějov and Kroměříž. Prostějov, 12 miles southwest of Olomouc, has a beautiful Renaissance town hall and the handsome **Church of the Holy Rood**. Also here is the baroque **Church of St. John** with an impressive Renaissance portal. Six miles west of town is the seventeenth-century **Plumlov castle** set on a picturesque lake. Kroměříž is best known for its baroque château, where you'll see a fine collection of paintings by the European masters. The seventeenth-century **Kroměříž French Park**, modeled after Versailles, is a great place to stroll in warm months. You can visit the greenhouse, music pavilion, and rotunda or walk along the grand colonnade crowned with statues of mythological figures. The historic district has another Renaissance town hall, as well as fine arcaded burghers' houses.

Finally, about three hours to the east in Slovakia is Trenčín, famed for its restored Roman castle. Its square tower, ancient town walls, and Renaissance homes make this city, Rome's northernmost base in central Europe, a treat. An inscription in the castle, commemorating an A.D. 179 Roman victory, is the oldest written record in the nation. While the castle is the prime attraction, the Renaissance town square, home of the **Piarist Monastery and Church**, is also a delight. From Trenčín you can loop back to Prague via Bratislava or head east to Zvolen. To the north is Banská Bystrica, gateway to the Tatra mountain resorts. The road south leads to our Hungarian great cities.

Poland

Although Poland has been in the news constantly for the past dozen years, it remains something of a mystery to most Westerners. Free at last, the nation's valiant campaign against Soviet colonialism made a hero out of Solidarity leader and president, Lech Walesa. It even persuaded the United States to cancel half of Poland's huge debt. A kind of dowry for democracy, the support of the West has helped make Poland a symbol for the bright promise of Eastern Europe. At the same time, many Westerners still visualize the nation in black and white, or, if you will, gray. But those who characterize this nation as shabby, melancholy, and backward are often people who have never seen its great castles and town squares or its colorful folk art and dress, tried its fine restaurants, or, most important, met the lively and energetic Poles up close. In short, Poland is one of the most misunderstood countries in Eastern Europe.

Each year, several million visitors discover the special pleasures of Poland, a nation that has not, as yet, been subjected to mass tourism. If you are the kind of person who likes to visit a promising destination before it turns red hot, we urge you to put Poland on your itinerary. Especially now, a visit to Poland is much more than a holiday. It is an adventure, a chance to witness a dramatic period of democratization. The people behind this transition from a Socialist to a market economy are a delight. This was the first Eastern bloc nation to topple the Communists. Today, the Poles are making important economic sacrifices as they build the economic framework necessary to create a sound future. Although you may not find the kind of luxury that characterizes Western European cities, Poland remains a bargain. Right now, before inflation pushes prices closer to those of the prosperous West, is an excellent time to visit.

As you travel through this diverse country, you are likely to find many surprises. Poland is more than just a newly liberated Eastern European country. It also has a colorful and turbulent past that will take you back more than a thousand years. As you visit our recommended destinations, you will discover magnificent historical treasures that help explain the story of this nation that once stretched from the Baltic to the Black Sea.

The Poles are also well known for their hospitality and genuine interest in meeting foreigners. They will be the first to admit that their language is impossible, but you will find that many people speak English as well as German and French. As you make new friends, hear their stories, answer their questions, and see their beautiful cities, you are likely to become hooked on Poland. All this, plus the exciting political scene, just may start you thinking about a return visit before your first trip has ended.

In Warsaw, the capital city, you will find history intermingling with concrete problems of the present. In addition to being the political heart of the country, it is convenient to some of the nation's most important historical assets, ones you will not want to miss. Krakow is a must if you are interested in European history. Like Prague, this beautiful city miraculously avoided destruction in the Second World War. Today it is a UNESCO World Heritage Site and one of the few authentic old cities in Poland. Gdansk, a city constantly in the news over the past decade, is more than just the birthplace of Solidarity. This ancient European community has been beautifully restored and retains the atmosphere of a prosperous Renaissance harbor town.

The origins of the Polish state go back to 966. That was the year Poland adopted Christianity and entered the arena of European history. Converted by Rome, not the Orthodox Church of Constantinople, Poland was fated to look West, not East, for the next thousand years. It was deeply immersed in all the great movements of

Poland

Western culture—the Renaissance, the Reformation, the baroque, and so on.

Until the second half of the fourteenth century, Poland was ruled by the Piast dynasty and went through a succession of divisions, unifications, and wars with its neighbors. Poland's enviable location attracted migratory armies who constantly crossed the borders to ravage the country. In 1226, Conrad, Duke of Masovia, turned to the Order of Teutonic Knights, a German semi-religious society of knights and priests, to help him defeat Prussian invaders. The Teutonic knights annexed the province of Pomerania and settled the land with Germans, initiating a political struggle that continues to this day. During the fourteenth-century reign of King Kazimierz Wielki (Casimir the Great), Poland entered its "Golden Age," which lasted for 200 years. Arts and science flourished during this period, and the nation's first university was established at

Krakow in 1364. Poland became renowned across Europe for its religious tolerance and gave refuge to minorities, especially Jews, from across the continent. After the union with Lithuania, Poland was ruled by the Jagiellonian dynasty. One of the principle events of this period was the defeat of the Teutonic Knights at the great battle of Grunwald in 1410.

This period of splendor was followed by frequent wars with Tatars, Ukrainians, and Swedes. In 1683, King Jan III Sobieski defeated the Ottoman Turks at Vienna and restored Poland to greatness. But at the end of the eighteenth century, conquered Poland was divided up between Prussia, Austria, and Russia. Another partition followed several decades later, and the country was partitioned a third time at the Congress of Vienna in 1815.

For over a century, Poland disappeared from the world map, as patriots fought ceaselessly to regain independence through insurrections and uprisings in all three occupied zones. Finally, in 1918, at the end of the World War I, Poland regained its sovereignty. Now it faced the problem of uniting three provinces, ruled for over a century by three occupying powers. Free from foreign domination and censorship, the next twenty years were a bright period in Polish history. Tragically, the hopes created by a democratic Poland were vanquished on September 1, 1939, when the Nazis launched their brutal invasion. Six million Poles, including nearly all the nation's Jews, lost their lives to Hitler's army during World War II.

Under socialism, this devastated land was completely rebuilt following the war. In August 1989, after nearly 45 years of harsh Communist rule, the Solidarity opposition defeated the ruling political monopoly. A vote heard around the world, this was the first victory of a non-Communist leader in the Iron Curtain countries. Since then, many significant political and economic changes, such as a free press and private ownership of businesses, have helped remake this nation. Today many new challenges lie ahead for the resilient and resourceful Poles. Come with us now as we take you backstage to see the story behind this historic political drama.

ARRIVAL
Poland is easily reached from all major European cities. Here are some of your options.

By Air: There are daily flights to Warsaw from most major Western European cities. LOT, the Polish Airlines, offers direct flights from New York and Chicago. In addition, you can reach the capital on Delta, Lufthansa, KLM, British Air, Malev, CSA, and many other carriers. Warszawa-Okecie International Airport is about 20 minutes from the city center. You can use the special bus transfer service (hourly from the airport to the Marriott Hotel in the center) or take a taxi. If you do the latter, take a registered taxi and inquire about the fare before you get in. Registered taxis at the airport have blue "Airport Taxi" stickers on them. Be careful of unregistered taxis. Although they also have a meter and the standard taxi sign, there is no limit on what you may be charged!

Domestic flights depart from another airport near Okecie at 17 Stycznia Street. You will connect here if you are flying to Krakow or Gdansk.

By Rail: You can reach all the Polish cities in this book via rail. Both the Paris-Moscow and Hoek van Holland-Moscow express provide connections to these destinations. You will change at Poznan for Krakow and Gdansk. The Warsaw-Krakow service is swift and efficient, taking only three hours. In the capital, you will use the Warszawa Centralna station at #54 Al. Jerozolimskie. Tel. 365/007. To avoid lines, it is a good idea to purchase your train tickets in advance at #16 ul. Bracka. Tel. 277/261. This city ticket office is located in the Orbis building. The round-trip rail ticket from Warsaw to Krakow is about 180,000 zloty ($18). The Warsaw-Gdansk round-trip is 200,000 zloty ($20).

By Car: Poland is easily reached from Germany and Czechoslovakia. If you wish to travel to Poland by car, make sure you have an international driver's license and an insurance policy for civil liability that also covers Poland. Rental cars can be arranged with companies like Hertz and Avis through Orbis travel offices. Budget also offers very competitive rates. Check with them at the Warsaw airport or the Marriott Hotel downtown.

Car rentals average around $50 a day. Advance reservations are a good idea. If you require assistance in the event of your car breaking down, call PZM Bureau of Motor Tourism, #63 Al. Jerozolimskie. Tel. 286/251. For your protection, park your car at a hotel garage overnight. Do not leave valuables in your vehicle.

Royal Castle, Warsaw, Poland

Bear in mind that unleaded gas (*Benzyna bezolowiu*) is not available everywhere. Here is a partial list of stations that do offer unleaded. A complete list is available from any ADAC auto club office in Germany. Remember to buy your gas before 6:00 p.m., and never travel with less than half a tank.

City	Station
Bialystok	Dojlidy
Bielsko-Biala	Cieszynska
Brodnica	Sikorskiego
Bydgoszsz-Bromberg	Dzierzynskiego
Czestochoma-Tschenstochau	Warszawska
Gdansk-Danzog	Dabrowskiego
Gdansk-Orunia	Jednosci Robotniczej
Katowice	Rozdzienskiego
Kolbaskowo	Grenzubergang
Krakow	Koniewa
Lublin	Krasnicka
Lodz	Tersy
Poznan	Warszawska
Slupsk	Baltycka
Warsaw	Emilii Plater Czerniakowska
Wroclaw-Breslau	Slezna
Zakopane	Richtg. Ustupie

MONEY

The Polish currency is the zloty, convertible at approximately 10,000 zloty to one U.S. dollar. Money can be changed at foreign exchange counters called *kantor wymiany*. They are usually closed on weekends. In higher category hotels, you can settle your bills directly in dollars.

TELEPHONE

As with all calls from the United States, you must first dial 011 for international long distance, then dial the country code followed by the city code and number. The country code for Poland is 48. City codes relevant to this book are Warsaw (22), Krakow (12), and

Gdansk (58). Remember to put a 0 in front of the area code when you are calling long distance within the country. If you are calling 675-453 in Warsaw from the United States, here is how to dial: 011-48-22-675-453. It is difficult to make long distance calls back home. Your best bet is to try to place the call through a hotel operator.

Warsaw

Warsaw, the capital of Poland, lies in the heart of Europe at the junction of major East-West air, rail, and land routes. This city of 1.7 million flanks Poland's longest river, the Wisla. Warsaw is an intriguing metropolis full of colorful streets, historical monuments, art galleries, theaters, museums, fine shops, and parks. While it is certainly not the most beautiful city in Europe, it is an excellent hub, convenient to many of the nation's most desirable destinations. Moderate prices make it an excellent bet for the budget-minded traveler. And the capital is at the center of a fascinating political scene, one that has attracted academics, journalists, and tourists from all over the world.

During the Second World War, Hitler condemned Warsaw to total destruction. When the Germans abandoned the city in 1945, they left behind them a cemetery: 85 percent of the capital was in ruins. As you walk through the streets of Warsaw, there is little left to remind you of this tragedy. The city has been completely restored, the old historical monuments lovingly rebuilt. The Old Town complex with its Renaissance and baroque houses is a magnificent example of the meticulous restoration of this city. As you stroll down the Krakowskie Przedmiescie past the magnificent palaces of old Polish aristocratic families, the historical churches, and the monuments, you will be impressed by the dedication and skill of the artists and artisans who rebuilt Warsaw.

GETTING AROUND
Warsaw has an extensive network of buses and trams. Bus tickets must be bought in advance in Ruch kiosks and validated on the bus. As the bus fares vary and there is often no information about the

Old Town Market Square, Warsaw, Poland

route at the bus stop itself, get all the necessary information from your hotel. Taxis are still relatively inexpensive and a good way of getting around. But be careful! Inquire about the fare before you get in, and use registered taxis only. Radio taxis can be booked by telephone (tel. 22-919). You can also find them outside hotels and railway stations and at taxi stands.

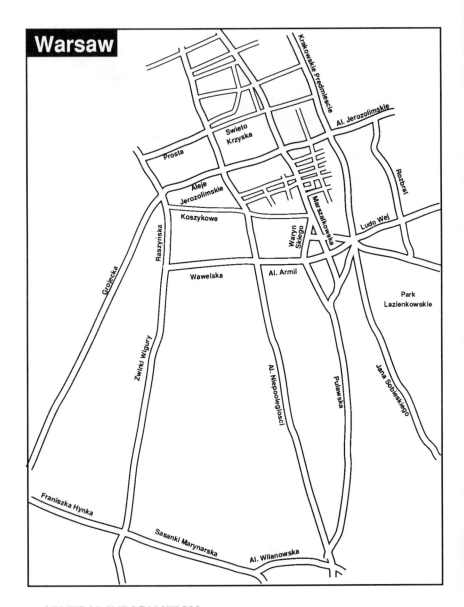

GENERAL INFORMATION

Start by going to the **Tourist Information** office (IT) in Old Town at #1/13 Plac Zamkowy. Tel. 270–000. It is open Monday through Friday 9:00 a.m. to 6:00 p.m., Saturday and Sunday 10:00 a.m. to

4:00 p.m. Here you will find maps of the city, information on sight-seeing tours and current events, and a list of cheaper hotels and bed and breakfasts currently available in Warsaw. An English-speaking guide can be arranged through **Juventur Travel Agency** at #27/31 ul. Gdanska. Tel. 330-041. Formerly a state agency for youth tourism, it now offers a broad range of services. Intriguing Warsaw sightseeing tours are organized by Poltur Ltd. at #9 ul. Etiudy Rewolucyjnej. Tel. 485-505. The National Tourist Agency, **Orbis**, still has the largest network of offices in Poland and offers the largest variety of services to the individual tourist. Contact their office at #142 ul. Marszalkowska. Tel. 635-7123. You may also want to visit some of the new private tourist offices springing up in Warsaw every week.

LODGING

If you want to stay in a four- or five-star hotel in Warsaw, book well in advance. Expect to pay prices comparable to those charged in Western Europe. The prices range from about 750,000 zloty ($75) to 1.6 million zloty ($160) for a double room. While service is excellent, you may notice some differences between Warsaw's deluxe establishments and those in the West. Telephone service remains spotty. At one point, owners of one of the city's new luxury hotels were talking about communicating with smoke signals sent up from the roof.

All of our recommended hotels are in the center of Warsaw within short walking distance of the Old Town or the center. In the 1,600,000 zloty-a-night range ($160) is the **Victoria Intercontinental Hotel** at #11 Krolewska. Tel. 278-011. The **Hotel Europejski** at #13 ul. Krakowskie Przedmiescie runs about 900,000 zloty ($90). Tel. 265-051. The **Hotel Polonia** at #45 Al. Jerozolimskie runs 750,000 zloty ($75). Tel. 628-7241.

More moderately priced hotels often come with a shared bath in Warsaw. The **Dom Chlopa** at #9 Pl. Powstancow Warszawy runs 370,000 zloty ($37). Tel. 279-251. **Hotel Saski**, #1 Pl. Bankowy, runs about 300,000 zloty ($30). Tel. 204-611. The **Dom Turysty**, #4/6 ul. Krakowski Przedmiescie, offers rooms for 260,000 zloty ($26). Tel. 260-071.

If you want to get a close-up view of day-to-day homelife, stay in a private apartment. The price of a double room is about

Village store, Stanislowo, Poland, north of Warsaw

130,000 zloty ($13). These private rooms can be booked through **Syrena**, #17 ul. Krucza (tel. 217-864), which is open daily except Sunday 8:00 a.m. to 8 p.m. If you are considering a homestay, use an office such as Syrena to make sure potential hosts meet your standards. This is one of the best ways we know to make new friends in Poland. Check carefully on the location: some private rooms are inconveniently situated far from the city center. Make sure the renting agency confirms by telephone that the host will meet you on arrival.

The **Polish Tourist Association** (PTTK) runs a chain of budget hotels and hostels usually in the one- or two-star category. Accommodations are simple but adequate for the budget traveler. Most of your fellow guests will be Poles. For information, contact the association at #36 ul. Swietokrzyska. Tel. 208-241.

Almatur, the Polish Student's Travel Association, also offers cheap accommodations for students and people under 35 in their chain of International Students Hostels. For information, visit their office at #9 ul. Ordynacka. Tel. 262-356. Almatur hostels, open from July 1 to September 15, are located at #4/6 Miedzyparkowa (tel. 311-766) and #397 Wal Miedzeszynski (tel. 178-851). Camping is available in the summer months at **Balaton-WOW Wisla**, #5 ul. Balaton. Tel. 344-213.

FOOD

As with hotels, restaurants are divided into five categories—from "lux" to Category IV. We suggest the higher categories unless you get a good local recommendation. All of our recommendations are Category I or lux. Polish food is hearty—roast meats, dumplings, cream sauces, and thick soups. If you are visiting Poland in summer you will find *chlodnik* offered in all restaurants. This is a delicious cold soup, made with red beets and cream. Also try the famous *barszcz* (borscht) or some *zrazy* (thin slices of beef cooked with onions). Traditionally, vodka is ordered with meals, but wines and beers are also available. When dining out in Poland, bear in mind that dinner is eaten early here. If you want to enjoy a leisurely meal, try to arrive before 7:00 p.m. Many restaurants close at 10:00 p.m. and stop serving hot dishes about 9:00 p.m.

The Poles love café life, meeting their friends and talking over coffee and cakes. The variety of cakes is enormous. Try a *szarlotka* (apple cake) or a *Wuzetka* (chocolate and cream cake). Most cafés close at 10:00 p.m. For a late evening drink, go to one of the hotel bars or all-night snack bars.

As state-owned restaurants and cafés switch to private owner-ship, you will find that service and quality are improving. These noisy establishments are social hubs and an excellent place to get to know the Poles. Chances are they may even come up and introduce themselves. Most restaurants and cafés close at 11:00 p.m. The expensive **Pod Bazyliszkiem** (Old Town Square) serves excellent food—traditional Polish dishes as well as international cuisine. Tel. 311-841. On Old Town Square in the same price range is **Fukier**. Tel. 313-918. The **Cristal-Budapeszt** at #21/25 Marszalkowska Street specializes in Hungarian food. Tel. 253-433. Prices here are moderate. Another good value for traditional Polish fare is the **Karczma Slupska** at #127 Czerniakowska. The reception desk at your hotel will be able to give you an update on this constantly changing scene and advise you on new restaurants.

If you're visiting Wilanow Castle (see Sightseeing, below), try the reasonably priced **Kuznia Krolewska** at #2 ul. Wiertnicza. The menu features traditional Polish food. For moderately priced Polish and international food, try **Adria** at #8 ul. Moniuszki. Tel. 274-240. **Sofia**, at #3/5 Plac Powstancow Warszawy, is known for its inexpensive Bulgarian dishes. Tel. 271-693. An interesting place for a quick and very inexpensive meal, as well as local color, is one of the state-run milk bars (*bar mleczny*). In these vegetarian establishments, you will find many dishes prepared with milk and dairy products. Try **Bar Mleczny Uniwersytecki** at #20 Krakowskie Przedmiescie.

Warsaw cafés we like include the **Krokodyl** at Rynek Starego Miasta (tel. 314-427), the **Rozdroze** at #6 Al. Ujazdowskie, and the **Ambasador** at #4 ul. Matejki (tel. 211-158).

NIGHTLIFE

Apart from many cozy little restaurants and cafés in Old Town, you will find Warsaw does not have extensive night life. Among the possibilities is the **Akwarium Jazz Club** at #2 ul. Emilii Plater. One of the most famous student clubs in Warsaw is **Stodola** at #10 ul. Batorego, where you will find disco dancing, concerts, and theater.

OPERA/CLASSICAL MUSIC

The **National Theater for Opera and Ballet** is located at Plac Teatralny. Tel. 263-287. You can hear the **National Philharmonic** at #12 ul. Sienkiewicza. Tel. 265-712. Tickets for all events and performances can be booked in advance through **Spatif** at #25 Al. Jerozolimskie. Tel. 219-454.

SHOPPING

Food stores are usually open from 6:00 a.m. to 7:00 p.m. (on Saturdays only until 1:00 p.m.). All other shops open at 11:00 a.m. and close at 7:00 p.m. For Polish handicrafts, visit the Cepelia shops at #2 and #5 Pl. Konstytucji or #8/10 Rynek Starego Miasta. Here you'll find a large selection of ceramics and embroidered, hand-woven, or carved objects. For unique handmade silver products, try Orno at #52 ul. Nowy Swiat. In Warsaw's Old Town, you will find many small shops and galleries offering leather goods, jewelry, and paintings.

Old Town Market Square, Warsaw

SIGHTSEEING

Cynics say the best place to start sightseeing in Warsaw is from the top of the **Palace of Culture and Science**, a towering piece of Stalinist architecture in the center of the city. Besides offering an unforgettable view of Warsaw, this is the only place in town where you cannot see the palace itself. For many Poles, this monumental 30-story building (one of the highest in Europe) dominating the Plac Defilad (Parade Square) is a blight on the landscape. It was presented by the Soviet Union to the Polish nation in the early 1950s, a fact that may explain why it is currently suffering from neglect. Appropriately, the Polish Communist party was buried at its final annual congress here in January 1990.

Old Town

Start off your tour of Old Town at the **Warsaw Historical Museum** (Muzeum Warszawy) located on Old Town Square at #28 Rynek Starego Miasta. Tel. 310-251. Here you will find seven carefully documented centuries of Warsaw history. It offers surprising

Old Town Market Square, Warsaw

insights into the city's past. Another good reason to visit the museum is a 20-minute film documenting the methodical World War II destruction of Warsaw. It is spliced together from German newsreels. This shocking movie will help you appreciate the dedication and sacrifice required to reconstruct the city following the war. The museum is open Tuesday and Thursday from noon to 7:00 p.m. and Wednesday, Friday, and Saturday from 10:30 a.m. to 4:30 p.m. Call 310-251 for information and the film schedule.

After leaving the museum, you will find yourself in **Old Town Square**. With its re-created Renaissance and baroque houses, colored in ochre, gold, and green, this is one of Warsaw's loveliest spots. The original buildings were the homes of noblemen and wealthy merchants. Their status could be gauged by the number of windows and the intricacy of the facade designs. Take a walk down the picturesque little streets surrounding the square. You will find lovely courtyards, houses, monuments, plenty of little art galleries, cafés, and lots of colorful street life. Behind the medieval fortifications of the city lies the New Town (Nowe Miasto) with its gentle atmosphere and graceful seventeenth- and eighteenth-century houses.

Here at #16 Freta Street you will find the **Birthplace of Maria Sklodowska**. Married to Pierre Curie, Madame Curie became an outstanding chemist and physicist—honored twice with the Nobel Prize for her work with radium. The museum is open Tuesday through Saturday from 10:00 a.m. to 4:30 p.m. and Sunday from 10:00 a.m. to 2:30 p.m. Tel. 318-092. On this street you'll also want to take a look at the **Church of the Sisters of the Blessed Sacrement** (Kosciol Sakramentek) in New Town Square (Rynek Nowego Miasta) built by King Jan III Sobieski in 1688 to commemorate his victory over the Turks at Vienna.

As you walk back through Old Town toward Castle Square (Plac Zamkowy) you will pass the oldest church in Warsaw, the **Cathedral of St. John** (Katedra Swietego Jana), originally built in the thirteenth and fourteenth centuries, where coronations of Polish kings took place and where many famous Poles are buried, among them Nobel Prize-winner Henryk Sienkiewicz, the author of *Quo Vadis*. The cathedral was the scene of some of the bloodiest and most bitter fighting in the Warsaw Uprising of 1944. Completely destroyed, it has been rebuilt in the Gothic style typical of the Wisla region.

In the center of **Castle Square** stands Warsaw's oldest monument—a tall, slender column with a statue of King Sigismund III on top. This honor is rightfully his for he was the king who moved the capital of the country from Krakow to Warsaw in 1596. The **Royal Castle** at #4 Plac Zamkowy has been the official royal residence since that time. Built between the fourteenth and eighteenth centuries, the castle was the birthplace of Polish democracy. Here the Constitution of the 3rd of May, second in the world after the U.S. Constitution, was written. Plundered of its treasures by the Nazis during World War II, it was finally blown to bits at the end of 1944. After the war, the castle was carefully reconstructed and now houses priceless treasures from all over the world. Many were donated by countries eager to show their solidarity with the Polish people. English-language guided tours are available at the Royal Castle on request. The castle is open Tuesday through Saturday from 10:00 a.m. to 2:30 p.m. Tel. 319-199.

The Royal Tract

As you stand on Castle Square, you are looking toward one of the most beautiful streets in Warsaw, **Krakowskie Przedmiescie.** Lined with eighteenth-century palaces, churches, and monuments, it recaptures the city's Old World elegance. Each building has a rich history, and you can spend hours wandering in and out of the churches, looking into palace courtyards, and admiring architectural details of the palaces. This is the street where Frederic Chopin grew up. As a young boy, he played the organ at the **Church of the Nuns of the Visitation** (Kosciol Wizytek). His heart is buried on Krakowskie Przedmiescie, according to his wishes, in an urn at the Church of the Sacred Heart.

Nowy Swiat is a continuation of Krakowskie Przedmiescie, a bustling, lively street of a more commercial character. If you continue down Nowy Swiat, you will eventually come to **Al. Ujazdowskie,** an elegant old Warsaw street that is now the heart of the city's government and diplomatic sector. To your left stretches Warsaw's main park—**Lazienki**—an eighteenth-century landscape garden. Set on an island within the park is the lovely **Lazienki Palace,** the summer residence of Poland's last king, Stanislaw August Poniatowski. On Sunday at 11:00 a.m. you will hear the sound of piano music floating through the park. Free open-air concerts are held here in late spring, summer, and early fall. They take place under the Chopin Monument at the park's entrance. Lazienki Park and Lazienki Palace are open daily except Monday. The grounds are open 10:00 a.m. to dusk. The palace is open Tuesday through Sunday from 10:00 a.m. to 4:00 p.m. Tel. 218-212.

The Royal Tract continues down **Belwederska Street,** named after Belvedere Palace (on your left), the seat of the president of Poland. It runs on for several miles all the way to Wilanow, a residential palace built by King Jan III Sobieski. **Wilanow Palace** on ul. Wiertnicza is a fine example of Polish baroque architecture. Now a museum, it has a beautiful collection of old Polish portraits well worth visiting. Wilanow Palace is open Wednesday through Monday from 9:30 a.m. to 2:30 p.m. The park remains open until 5:00 p.m. Tel. 420-795.

Next to the palace at #1 ul. Wiertnicza, you will find the world's first **Poster Museum.** Polish posters have won many international awards. Be sure to see the remarkable collection here. This museum is open Tuesday through Sunday from 10:00 a.m. to 4:00 p.m. Tel. 422-606.

The Warsaw Ghetto

From Old Town, walk through the Barbican to Freta Street and turn into Swietojerska Street, which will lead you past the palace of the Krasinski family, a seventeenth-century baroque landmark that is now the **National Library**. Across the street is the new **Monument to the Heroes of the Warsaw Uprising** of 1944. Take a closer look: you will be touched by the symbolism of the figures that appear to be rising from the building ruins. In August 1944, Warsaw's civilian populace, led by remnants of the Polish army of 1939, rose up against the occupying Germans. The uprising lasted for two months and large sections of the town were liberated. In October 1944, the Germans finally crushed the insurrection and proceeded to methodically destroy the city. Roughly 150,000 Poles died in the uprising, 50,000 were sent to concentration camps, and another 150,000 were forced into slave labor for the German Reich. Eighty-five percent of the city was destroyed.

Swietojerska Street will lead you to **Mordechaja Anielewicza Street** and the **Jewish Ghetto**. The street is named after the young commander of the Ghetto Uprising of 1943. During World War II, Jews from Warsaw and surrounding areas were herded into the ghetto, which was completely cut off from the rest of the town by a high wall. About 500,000 Jews lived here at the mercy of the Nazis. Starvation and disease took thousands of lives each month, and in summer 1942, transfers to the death camp at Treblinka began at a rate of more than 5,000 Jews a day. The uprising was a last ditch attempt to halt the Third Reich's slaughter. After putting down the uprising, the Germans turned the ghetto into one of Hitler's ghost towns, executing the remaining Jews or deporting them to concentration camps. They also symbolically blew up the Jewish Synagogue. Polish Jews, who at the turn of the century made up nearly 50 percent of Warsaw's population, were virtually extinct by the war's end. The Ghetto Uprising ended in Zamenhoff Street, where you'll find a monument commemorating the heroes of the ghetto. Designed by Nathan Rappaport, it was made out of a block of stone the Germans

Royal Castle, Warsaw

intended to use for the base of a Hitler monument.

Continue walking down Anielewicza Street until you reach the old Jewish cemetery. If you would like to find out more about the Ghetto Uprising and Polish Jewry, visit the **Jewish Historical Institute** at #3/5 Tlomackie Street. It is open Monday through Friday from 9:00 a.m. to 3:00 p.m.

Around Warsaw

A local bus can take you west 36 miles to Chopin's birthplace, **Zelazowa Wola.** But we recommend joining one of the coach excursions organized by Orbis or PTTK to make sure you enjoy a Chopin recital usually performed by some of Poland's finest pianists. Although Chopin was less than a year old when he left Zelazowa Wola, he returned here often, and his music reflects the moods of the surrounding countryside as well as the peasant tunes of this district. The house is actually a small cottage, beautifully reconstructed and appointed with period furniture and Chopin memorabilia. Be sure to visit the museum dedicated to the composer's life. Tel. 828-22300.

For more information about Zelazowa Wola, contact the Chopin Society in Warsaw at #1 ul. Okolnik. The society is closed on Sundays. Tel. 275-471.

Krakow

A city of 750,000, proud of its traditions and heritage, the home of the pope and one of Europe's great cultural treasures, Krakow is Poland at its best. It is the kind of place where you come for the day and stay for the week. The entire old town qualifies as a museum. Krakow is the third largest city in Poland and lies on the Upper Wisla, about 180 miles south of Warsaw. Poland's former

capital, it is a city that miraculously escaped destruction in World War II. Preserved in its entirety as a medieval town, Krakow's thirteenth-century layout is a pedestrian's delight. The historic center, where cars are prohibited, is an architectural shrine. Within the city you will find over 140 churches, more than 5,500 old burghers' houses, and roughly two million first-class works of art.

Since 1978, historic Krakow has been on the United Nations list of the world's top dozen World Heritage Sites. As you explore this fascinating city, you'll understand why it is both a religious and a cultural shrine. It is also front and center in the nation's new political order. Eager to help retire the nation's vast national debt accumulated by the Communists, students here took up a collection and sent the proceeds to the new government in Warsaw. From its

Sunday used car flea market to its venerable old student cafés, Krakow is a city full of delightful surprises. Enjoy them as you explore one of Eastern Europe's great finds.

GETTING THERE

The easiest way to reach Krakow is by express train from Warsaw. The journey takes about three hours. You can also travel to Krakow by bus or plane. If you prefer to take a guided tour, contact Orbis at #142 ul. Marszalkowska in Warsaw (tel. 273-673) or Poltur Ltd. at #9 ul. Etiudy Rewolucyjnej (tel.485-505).

For maps and current information about Krakow, contact the Tourist Information Center at #8 ul. Pawia. Tel. 226-091.

LODGING

Since more than two million tourists visit Krakow each year, it is necessary to make advance hotel reservations, particularly in the peak season. You can contact the hotels directly or use the services of Wawel-Tourist Hotel Reservation Services at #6 ul. Pawia. Tel. 224-162. This office is open daily from 9:00 a.m. to 3:00 p.m.

Your best bet is a hotel in the Old Town area. **Hotel "Pod Roza"** at #14 ul. Florianska offers double rooms for about 550,000 zloty ($55). Tel. 229-399. **Hotel Francuzki** at #13 ul. Pijarska has

Apostles, Church of Saints Peter and Paul, Krakow, Poland

double rooms for about 500,000 zloty ($50). Tel. 225-270. The **Hotel Polski** at #17 ul. Pijarska offers rooms for about 365,000 zloty ($37). Tel. 221-144. Away from the Old Town area are two hotels in the 650,000 to 950,000 zloty range ($65 to $95). They are the **Hotel Cracovia** at #1 Al. Puszkina (tel. 228-666) and the **Hotel Holiday Inn** at #7 ul. Koniewa. Tel. 375-044.

It is also possible to book private rooms through the Wawel Tourist Office at #8 ul. Pawia. Call 221-921. The earlier you arrive, the better your chances of finding a place to stay. Unfortunately, these rooms are usually inconveniently located away from the center of town. **Almatur** also has hostel accommodations in the summer months. Their office is at #7 Rynek Glowny. Tel. 226-352. Hours are Monday through Friday, 10:00 a.m. to 1:00 p.m. and 2:00 p.m. to 4:00 p.m. If you are calling long distance, the Krakow area code is 12. Within Poland, add a 0 before calling long distance.

FOOD

Krakow is a very lively city and prides itself on being just as much a Polish cultural capital as Warsaw. You will find it full of busy cafés and restaurants, theaters, cabarets, concerts, and dancing. For Polish food, try **Hawelka** at #24 Rynek Glowny. Tel 224-753. Another good possibility is **Staropolska** at #4 ul. Sienna. Tel. 225-821. Do not miss **Wierzynek** at #15 Rynek Glowny. Tel. 221-035. It is reputed to be the best restaurant in Poland.

As restaurants are sold to private owners, prices are rising steadily. Expect to pay only slightly less than you would in Western Europe for your meal.

Cafés

The late afternoon is the best time to head for coffee and cakes at one of Krakow's cafés. You will certainly find the rest of the town there. Do not miss the **Jama Michalikowa** at #45 ul. Florianska. Once famous for its cabaret, this historic café is furnished with fine antiques, hand-carved mantles, and gilded mirrors. We consider it a museum of the Krakow good life. A good bet for the evening is **Piwnica pod Baranami** at #27 Rynek Glowny or **Klub pod Jaszc-zurami**, down the street at #18 Rynek Glowny.

St. Sigismund Chapel, Wawel Cathedral, Krakow, Poland

SIGHTSEEING

Now that you're here, why not enter the old city as kings did in centuries past. Start your visit at the **Barbican** and the beautiful **Florian Gate** (Brama Florianska erected it in 1300), all that remain of the original wall that encircled the city's historic center. These fortifications were replaced 150 years ago by beautiful gardens. Straight ahead lies the Main Town Square (Rynek Glowny). Behind it, you will see **Wawel Hill** crowned by the **Royal Castle** complex. Walking down Florianska Street, note the intricate detailing on the home facades. Frequently they give you a capsule history of each building. For example, #24, which features three bells on its coat of arms, was for centuries the workshop and living quarters of a family of bell makers. Florianska Street opens into the Main Town Square, one of the most magnificent squares in the world. With its historic buildings and churches, flower stalls, street artists, vendors, and horse-drawn carriages, this square is a romantic place that you will want to explore at a leisurely place. Shop for a painting, chat with students eager to practice their English, look for souvenirs, and enjoy a cup of coffee in an elegant Old World café. When you're ready, head off to explore some of the city's world-class sights.

The Main Town Square

The Main Town Square (Rynek Glowny) has several outstanding monuments beginning with the Sukiennice or **Cloth Hall**. It was built in the fourteenth century, destroyed by fire in the sixteenth century, and rebuilt in the Renaissance style. Walking down the hall, you will find it cut in half by a passageway. On the wall, you'll see a blunt iron knife hanging from a chain. According to local legend, this knife is connected with the building of the nearby **Church of St. Mary** (Kosciol Mariacki) located in front of you on the square. The church was supposedly built by two brothers. The elder was a hard worker and his spire grew quickly. The younger, envious of his brother's progress, took this knife and killed him. Filled with remorse, he climbed the taller tower, confessed his crime, and stabbed himself with the same knife before jumping to his death. True or not, two things are certain. The knife still hangs from a chain

TOP: *Victory Column, Berlin, Germany (Courtesy InterMarketing Berlin)*

BOTTOM: *Berlin at night (Courtesy German National Tourist Office)*

POKLADŇA

DETSKÁ MANEŽ 2Kčs
LABUTE : DETI 3Kčs DOSPELÍ 3Kčs

FACING PAGE

UPPER LEFT: *Street scene, Slovakia, Czechoslovakia*

UPPER RIGHT: *Near Terezin, southern Bohemia, Czechoslovakia*

BOTTOM: *Carnival, Moravia, Czechoslovakia*

THIS PAGE

UPPER LEFT: *Prague, Czechoslovakia*

UPPER RIGHT: *Old Town Hall clock, Prague*

BOTTOM: *Jewish Cemetery in Prague's Josefov*

THIS PAGE

UPPER LEFT:
*Fisherman's
Bastion, Budapest,
Hungary*

UPPER RIGHT:
*Ezstergom,
Hungary*

BOTTOM: *Budapest,
Hungary*

FACING PAGE

UPPER LEFT:
*Pharmacy in
Sopron, Hungary*

UPPER RIGHT:
*Szentendre,
Hungary (Courtesy
Ibusz, Hungarian
Travel Company)*

BOTTOM LEFT:
Szirak, Hungary

BOTTOM RIGHT:
*Visegrad, on the
Danube Bend,
Hungary (Courtesy
Ibusz, Hungarian
Travel Company)*

FACING PAGE

UPPER LEFT:
Krakow, Poland

UPPER RIGHT:
*Farm near
Stanislowo, Poland*

BOTTOM: *Warsaw,
Poland*

THIS PAGE

UPPER LEFT: *Old
Town, Gdansk,
Poland (Courtesy
Polish National
Tourist Office)*

UPPER RIGHT:
*Long Market Street,
Gdansk, Poland
(Courtesy Polish
National Tourist
Office)*

BOTTOM:
*Dubrovnik,
Yugoslavia*

Upper left:
Dresden, Germany

Upper right:
Weimar, Germany

Bottom: *Dresden, Germany*

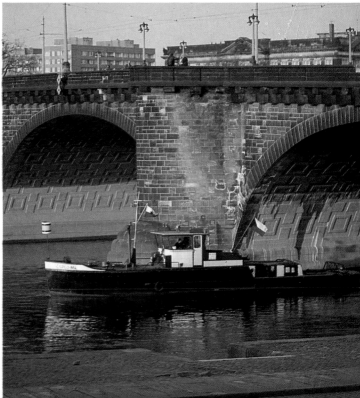

at the Cloth Hall, and the two towers of the Church of St. Mary's are different heights.

The Church of St. Mary's

This is Krakow's most important church, dating back to the late fourteenth century. The city's most powerful and wealthiest families all had their chapels here. As you go in, your eye will immediately be caught by one of Poland's finest works of art, the great **Triptych Altar of Wit Stwosz.** This is a magnificent late medieval wooden altarpiece, the largest Gothic wooden altar in Europe. The exquisite figures of the altar are life-sized and carved so realistically they almost seem alive. Memorable fourteenth-century stained glass windows are also found here.

As you walk around the church and the Main Town Square you may hear the silvery notes of a trumpet coming from the church tower. This is the **Hejnal,** a trumpet call, traditionally played every hour on the hour from the taller tower of St. Mary's Church. The call always ends abruptly on a high note. Tradition has it that thirteenth-century Tatar raiders once entered the city while people were at worship. They were spotted by a trumpeter stationed in the church tower. He immediately sounded the alarm. One of the Tatar arrows pierced the trumpeter's throat, and he died a hero. Because of his courage, Krakow was saved. The Hejnal is played hourly in his memory and ends in the same abrupt fashion. At noon, the Hejnal is broadcast over all Polish radio stations, a time when much of the nation pauses to set its clocks.

Leave the square by way of Grodzka Street, continuing down **Kanoniczna Street,** one of the city's most beautiful thoroughfares. It is lined with palaces and courtyards of wealthy merchants and noblemen. The view up Kanoniczna Street, with Wawel's pinnacles towering above houses distinguished by their richly ornamented doorways, is one of the best in Krakow.

Wawel Hill

Wawel Hill, the Royal Castle, and the cathedral offer a short lesson in Polish history. Here you will find the national past, its victories

Entryway to the Church of Saints Peter and Paul, Krakow, Poland

and defeats, its leaders and heroes. As you enter the Wawel complex, you will find rising to your left the bulk of the fourteenth-century Gothic **cathedral**, with its cluster of side chapels. This is where Polish kings were crowned and buried. In the vaulted crypt you will find, among others, the tombs of the Jagiello dynasty, the Waza dynasty, and King Jan III Sobieski. Buried here also are Polish national heroes like Tadeusz Kosciuszko, the great poet Adam Mickiewicz, and the statesman Marshall Pilsudski. Note the tomb of King Kazimierz Jagiellonczyk, another masterpiece by Wit Stwosz, the artist who created the altarpiece in the Church of St. Mary's.

There has been a royal castle on Wawel Hill since the tenth century, but the current castle dates from the sixteenth century when it was rebuilt as an early baroque residence. It was subsequently devastated by advancing Swedish, Prussian, and Austrian armies and, more recently, the Nazis. During the Second World War, it became the residence of the Nazi Gauleiter, Hans Frank. The Germans destroyed the royal stables and kitchens and looted many castle treasures.

There are four main exhibitions in the **Royal Castle**, all worth visiting. First, you'll want to see the **Royal Halls and Chambers** furnished in the style of the Jagiellonian and Waza dynasties. Here you will see the priceless collection of 143 tapestries from the sixteenth and seventeenth centuries. They are grouped by theme and decorate the chambers. Next, visit the **Royal Treasury**. The prize piece of the collection is the **Szczerbiec**, the coronation sword of Polish kings since 1320. In the **Royal Armoury**, there are over 500 exhibits, among them, the winged armor of King Jan III Sobieski's hussars and Turkish war trophies he brought back from Vienna. The **Eastern Collection** features one of the largest sets of seventeenth- and eighteenth-century Turkish and Persian tents in the world. Also here are rare Turkish flags, Persian carpets, and armor. The castle is open from 10:00 a.m. to 3:30 p.m. Tuesday through Sunday. Tel. 225-155.

Around Krakow

WIELICZKA
About 9 miles southeast of Krakow, easily reached by bus, are the amazing salt mines of Wieliczka. Salt has been mined here since the tenth century. In 1950, the oldest section of the mine was turned into a museum and became a major tourist attraction. Of the 120 miles of tunnels, galleries, and corridors underground, 2.5 miles are now open to the public. A guided tour takes about 3 hours and includes spectacular sights. Several chapels have been carved out of the salt. Tunnels open into unexpected vast chambers with walls, ceilings, floors, altars, and chandeliers all made of glittering salt crystals. You will also see mysterious salt lakes and even a tennis court. The mines, located at #20 ul. Danilowicza, are open from April 15 to October 21 from 9:00 a.m. to 7:00 p.m. daily. The rest of the year they are open from 8:00 a.m. to 3:00 p.m.

AUSCHWITZ-BIRKENAU (OSWIECIM-BRZEZINKA)
Located 30 miles west of Krakow, Oswiecim is known to the whole world by its German name, Auschwitz. It is easily reached by train from Krakow. In 1940, the Nazis established their largest concentration camp complex, Auschwitz-Birkenau. The local Polish

population was moved from this area and the camp surrounded by a no-man's-land more than a mile wide. According to evidence presented at the Nuremberg trials, about four million people were slaughtered here. The gas chambers of Birkenau were the standard by which all Nazi death camps were judged. At full tilt, they had capacity to kill 60,000 victims a day. Bodies were burned in cremation chambers and the ashes scattered in the nearby swamps. People from all over Europe, especially Jews, were murdered here, and today Auschwitz-Birkenau is the largest and most horrifying cemetery in the world.

The grounds of the camp have been turned into a museum. The concentration camp remains unchanged since the day the Nazis left it—prisoners' barracks and execution and cremation chambers are untouched and open for viewing. Auschwitz-Birkenau is a horrifying place, and understandably children are not allowed into its grounds. The state museum at #20 ul. Wiezniow is open June 1 through August 31 from 8:00 a.m. to 7:00 p.m. The rest of the year it is open 8:00 a.m. to 6:00 p.m.

Gdansk

Many famous European cities surround themselves with their past, eager to show you the glories of another era. But Gdansk is a classic example of living history and stands as a kind of Polish Lexington, the place where democracy came to stay. The cradle of the Independent Trade Union movement, "Solidarity," it was here that workers united to lead a seemingly impossible battle against Poland's Communist autocracy. The struggle started in the Gdansk shipyards, in 1980, following a wave of strikes all over the country. Lech Walesa, the union leader, became a national hero and ultimately Poland's democratically elected president.

But this is only the latest chapter in the story of this picturesque and famous city of 463,000. Poland's port since the Middle Ages, it

was a member of the Hanseatic League and the most prosperous port on the Baltic. Most of the city's famous monuments were built during its sixteenth- and seventeenth-century heyday. The city's growth was ultimately halted by the Swedish wars of the seventeenth century. Like the rest of Poland, control of Gdansk switched several times until finally, in 1919, it gained "free city" status under Polish rule. In 1938, Hitler demanded that Gdansk be given to Germany; Poland's refusal was used by Germany as a provocation for its September 1, 1939, attack on Poland. The first shots of World War II were fired here at Westerplatte. When liberated in March 1945, Gdansk was in ruins, the harbor devastated, its basin filled with sunken ships. As in Warsaw and many other cities devastated by the war, the city's leading monuments were lovingly restored. The result is an enchanting old town, with picturesque winding streets, lovely Renaissance and baroque house facades, and many impressive Gothic churches.

GETTING THERE

If you are traveling to Gdansk from Warsaw, take an express train from Warsaw Central Station. The journey takes approximately 4 hours. If you are traveling directly to Gdansk, take one of the international express trains from Ostend, Hoek van Holland, or Paris and change to a local express train in Poznan. There are also coach links from Warsaw and Poznan as well as LOT Polish Airlines flights from Warsaw.

LODGING

If you are planning a summer visit, be sure to reserve a hotel room well in advance. A good place to stay is the **Hotel Jantar** at #19 ul. Dlugi. Tel. 319-532. Rooms run about 200,000 zloty ($20). This hotel is ideally situated in the center of Old Town and moderately priced. In Gdansk but outside the Old Town area are a number of other hotels: the **Novotel** at #1 ul. Pszenna offers rooms for 480,000 zloty ($48), tel. 315-611; and **Hotel Heweliusz** at #22 ul. Heweliusza offers rooms for 540,000 zloty ($54), tel. 315-631.

If you wish to combine your sightseeing trip with a beach holiday, try one of the hotels in Gdansk-Jelitkowo. They are located within walking distance of Gdansk's beaches. The Old Town is also easily reached by bus. **Hotel Posejdon** in Gdansk-Jelitkowo at #30 ul. Kapliczna offers rooms for 490,000 zloty ($49). Tel. 531-803. **Hotel Marina-Orbis** in Gdansk-Jelitkowo, at #20 ul. Jeltkowska, offers rooms for 551,000 zloty ($55). Tel. 532-2079.

To arrange a private room, contact the **Biuro Zakwaterowania** at #10/11 Elzbietanska. Tel. 80-894. It is open from 7:30 a.m. to 7:00 p.m.

FOOD

The most popular restaurant in Gdansk is **Pod Lososiem**, at #51/54 ul. Szeroka. Tel. 317-652. This restaurant serves Polish food and some very good fish dishes. **Pod Wieza**, at #51 ul. Piwna, special-

Dlugi Targ, Neptune's Fountain and the Artusz Mansion, Gdansk, Poland

izes in Polish and international cuisine. Tel. 313-924. A good bet for seafood is **Retmann** at #1 ul. Stagiewna. Tel. 319-248. For dancing and cabaret, try the **Cristal** restaurant in Gdansk-Wrzeszcz at #105 ul. Grunwaldzka.

SIGHTSEEING

Start your sightseeing tour by visiting the Gdansk Tourist Information Center where you can pick up maps and get an update on nightlife and entertainment. It is located at #8 ul. Heweliusza. Tel. 315-63.

The Old Town

If you are traveling to Gdansk by train, you will arrive at the Main Train Station (Dworzec Glowny) just outside Old Town. This is the loveliest part of Gdansk, the ideal place to begin your visit. The two main Old Town streets are Dluga and Dlugi Targ, which form the **Royal Road**. Enter Old Town by the **High Gate** (Brama Wyzynna), which was the main city gate and forms part of the original Old Town fortifications. You will immediately enter **Dluga Street**, lined with historic merchants' houses featuring tall gables, airy windows, and handsome ornamentation. These palatial homes reflect the city's prosperity during its heyday (the 16th and 17th centuries). Midway along Dluga Street is the late Gothic **Old Town Hall** built in the fifteenth century. Inside, you will find the **Historic Museum of Gdansk**. While here, visit the exquisite Red Hall. The museum is located at #47 ul. Dluga. Tel. 316-119. It is open Tuesday from 10:00 a.m. to 3:30 p.m., Thursday from 10:00 a.m. to 4:00 p.m., Saturday from 2:00 p.m. to 5:30 p.m., and Sunday from 11:00 a.m. to 3:30 p.m.

Beyond the Town Hall stretches the loveliest part of Dluga with the Neptune Fountain and the Dwor Artusa, or **Arthur's Court**. One of the city's outstanding merchant houses, this residence served as a meeting hall for rich merchants.

The Motlawa River

Leave Old Town by the **Green Gate** (Zielona Brama) and walk to the Motlawa River. Ships from all over the world once docked at quays here. Although it now looks narrow, gray, and unspectacular, the river was the source of Gdansk's wealth in the sixteenth and seventeenth centuries. Across the bridge on **Granary Island** (Wyspa Spichrzow), two hundred big grain warehouses were protected by defense towers still visible today. As you walk along the Motlawa Quay you will see the Zuraw Gdanski, a medieval crane built in the fourteenth century. It doubled as part of the Gdansk fortifications. The **Motlawa Quay** is a lively section of old Gdansk. Little crafts shops, boutiques, and cafés flourish here. If you are interested in jewelry, you will find many small workshops here, The artists work with amber from the Baltic Sea, setting it into unique pieces of jewelry or carving it into ornamental objects.

St. Mary's Church

Retrace your steps and take the gateway into Mariacka Street, where you'll find more restored sixteenth-century houses. Continue to the small square and Poland's largest Gothic church—St. Mary's (Kosciol Najswietszej Marii Panny), begun in 1343 and finished in 1502. It can accommodate up to 25,000 worshipers.

You'll discover many other charming streets and sights in Gdansk as you stroll around Old Town. In the warm months, take a boat trip from the dock at the Green Gate. The steamer will take you around the port or downstream to Sopot. It will also take you past **Westerplatte**, the small peninsula where the Germans launched the attack that began World War II.

The Lenin Shipyards

Now that you have toured Gdansk's distant past, it is time to learn more about its recent history. At the Lenin Shipyards, you will find the monument to the memory of the Gdansk shipyard workers killed in 1970 street demonstrations. The monument is perfectly situated in front of the main gate, where the strikes of 1980 began. The independent trade union Solidarity was born during this walkout and won its first concessions from the Communist government. This labor struggle laid the groundwork for the political revolution that democratized Poland in 1989.

The monument consists of three gigantic black crosses with figures at the base. It is inscribed with a quote from the Polish poet and Nobel Prize winner, Czeslaw Milosz.

Outside Gdansk

SOPOT

One of the best day trips in the Gdansk area is a cruise from the dock near the Green Gate to Sopot. Here on the "Polish Riviera" there is an atmosphere of Edwardian elegance. The town's old villas and hotels are located in beautifully landscaped gardens. The broad beaches and long pier, the arrival point from Gdansk, are a popular weekend destination. A lively town, Sopot has excellent cafés, restaurants, dancing, and music. There's no better way to take a leisurely vacation from your vacation.

Hungary

If you've been dreaming of Turkey, thinking about Austria, wishing you were in Yugoslavia, or pining away for Italy, here is good news. Hungary, one of the most cosmopolitan nations in the world, a country that once stretched from the Adriatic to Transylvania, can give you a taste of all these cultures. For more than 1,000 years, Hungary has had one foot in Eastern Europe and the other in the West. From the Romans and the Magyars to the Hapsburgs and the Communists, this nation has always been at the crossroads of European politics, culture, art, and architecture. And although it is now only a third its pre-World War I size, its influence extends far beyond its own borders. Today it still has significant links with such countries as Poland, Germany, Austria, and Czechoslovakia. Over the centuries, many of the ruling powers of Europe have reconfigured this nation. And Hungarians living outside this nation's borders in regions like Romania's Transylvania continue to struggle against the political descendants of the Communists.

One of the first Iron Curtain nations to successfully woo capitalist interests, this nation has many signs of a country on the move. Budapest has many of the well-known European and American retail enterprises. Prosperous entrepreneurs can be seen driving about in their Mercedes sedans. And for those who demand the very best, it is possible to stay in castles that have been converted into first-class resorts.

For the visitor who wants a taste of Eastern Europe, without sacrificing many of the comforts one would expect in the West, Hungary is an excellent choice. The roads are good. At the foot of the Alps, Sopron and Köszeg are only a couple of hours from Vienna. Easily reached from Budapest, the Danube Bend towns of Szentendre, Visegrád, and Esztergom are the places to go for great architecture and religious art. And Eger, the gateway to Hungary's highest mountain range, is a pleasant retreat just two hours east of Budapest.

The capital city is also a delight, the kind of place where you are tempted to throw out your itinerary and settle in for as long as possible. Its world-class museums, monuments to St. Stephen, fairy tale castles, performing arts groups, and baths are well known. But this is also the kind of city where it is fun to simply walk around and sample baroque restaurants and Jewish monuments, cycle on a pastoral Danube island, or just linger for hours at a sidewalk café. Large pedestrian-oriented plazas and shopping districts, grand parks and festivals make the city a favorite getaway for Europeans. And if you have any interest in European architecture, this city is a must: from the Byzantine links of the Magyars to the glass-walled passive solar energy home in Pécs, Hungary showcases many important styles. Because it was heavily influenced by both the Eastern and Western European powers, the nation has an impressive variety of baroque, neoclassic, art nouveau, Gothic and neo-Renaissance buildings. If you're an archaeology buff, you will be glad to know that historic Roman castles and towns have been handsomely restored.

American visitors will definitely want to spend time exploring the backcountry. Because this is a small nation, most destinations are convenient to Budapest by train or car. This means that even if you have only a short time to visit Hungary, it is possible to enjoy both its urban and rural sides. Out of a vast number of excellent possibilities we have chosen several gems outside the capital that merit special consideration. Our selections are designed to give you a chance to sample the best at a comfortable pace. Follow this route and rest assured you are seeing the Hungary that many first-time visitors unfortunately miss. Because these destinations are three

A Pest trolley stop, Budapest, Hungary

hours or less by train, car, or hydrofoil from the capital, you can see a great deal without pushing yourself. As you explore this fascinating country, keep a flexible schedule, allowing time to meet the country's greatest asset, its people. A casual street corner conversation or a chance meeting on a train will offer insights beyond anything you have read or heard about this proud nation. Like the rest of Eastern Europe, this is a nation in transition, one immersed in the hard work of creating a democratic state that rights the wrongs of past rulers. You will find the Hungarians happy to share their complex and fascinating story.

ARRIVAL

Hungary is easily reached from all major European cities. Here are some of your options.

By Air: Budapest has Hungary's only commercial airport. **Ferihegy Airport 1** is served by international carriers such as Delta, KLM, CSA, and British Airways. **Ferihegy 2** is served only by MALEV, Hungary's national carrier, Lufthansa, and Air France.

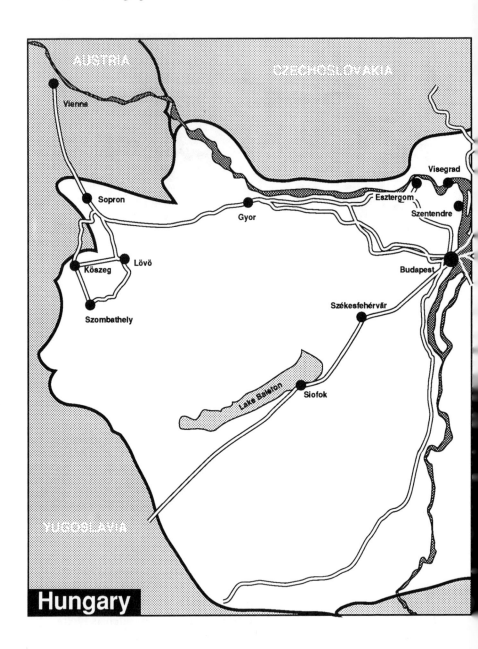

Hungary

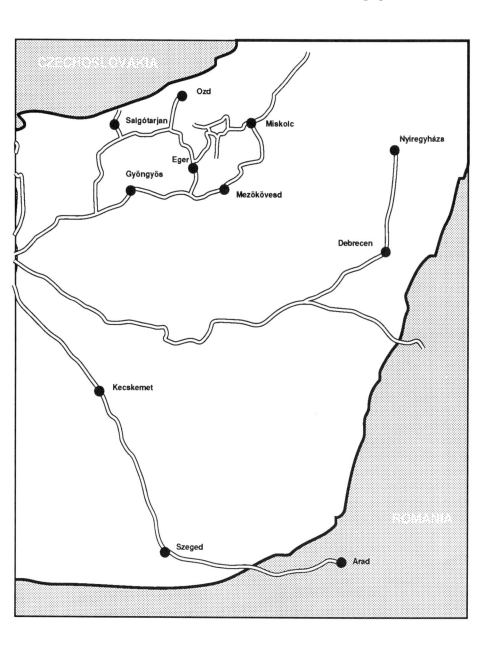

Entrance to the Royal Palace, now a museum complex on the Buda side of Budapest, Hungary

The two terminals, located four miles apart, are connected by a shuttle bus. Ferihegy 1 is 10 miles (30 minutes) from downtown Budapest, while Ferihegy 2 is 14 miles (40 minutes) away. There is direct bus service on the half hour from 6:00 a.m. to 10:00 p.m. between both airports and Erzsébet Square downtown. Taxis are available from both terminals.

By Train: The most popular way to reach Hungary, the Hungarian railroads offer convenient connections to all the destinations in this book. Sopron, just 40 miles from Vienna by rail, should be your first stop if you are beginning in western Hungary. From here, there is convenient bus service to Köszeg, 30 miles away. Budapest is about six hours from Vienna or Prague by rail. Eger is a 73-mile (2-hour) train ride from Budapest. For information, contact **MAV** passenger service at Andrássy #35. Tel. 118-2430.

By Bus: Direct bus service links Hungary with all major European destinations. There are two direct buses daily from Vienna to Budapest as well as service to more than thirty cities in Hungary. For information, contact **Volanbusz** at Erzsébet Square. Tel. 117-2562. In Vienna, call **Blaguss Reisen** at 651-681.

By Ship: Express hydrofoil service on the Danube links Budapest with Vienna. From April 1 through September 1, the vessels leave Vienna at 8:00 a.m. and arrive in Budapest at 1:30 p.m. The international pier is between Liberty and Erzsébet Bridge on the Pest side (left bank). There is also daily service between Budapest and Esztergom on the Danube Bend. For information, call **Mahart** at 118-1758 (international) or 118-1223 (domestic). In Vienna, you can book the Budapest hydrofoil for about $60 each way from **Ibusz Wein**. Tel. 532-686. In the United States, your travel agent can book the hydrofoil by calling **Hungarian Hotels Sales Office**, 6033 W. Century Boulevard, Suite 670, Los Angeles, CA 90045. Tel. (213) 649-5960 or (800) 448-4321.

By Car: The drive from Vienna to Sopron in western Hungary takes about two hours. From here it is about 40 minutes to Köszeg. The trip east to Budapest adds another three to four hours. From Prague to Budapest takes six to seven hours.

If you arrive by plane, train, or ship in Budapest, you will not need to rent a car to get around town. Public transit is excellent. But you may want a car for the trip to Sopron, Köszeg, the Danube Bend, or Eger. The speed limit is 120 km (75 mph) on motorways, 100 km (62 mph) on highways, 80 km (50 mph) on other roads, and 60 km (37 mph) in built-up areas. Hungarian police ticket aggressively, even for minor parking infractions. Foreigners are sometimes told to pay their fines on the spot. Drivers are not allowed to drink any alcohol prior to getting behind the wheel. A blood alcohol level over .008 can be grounds for arrest. Seat belt use is mandatory.

Although you can rent cars in Hungary, see the introduction to this book for suggestions on how to save money by booking your car in Germany or Austria.

Unleaded gas is available at the following locations:

BUDAPEST

Location

Meszaros #1

Fo út #66

Szabadsag tér

Kerepesi #5-7

Boldizsar u.

M3 Motorway

OTHER CITIES

Location

Debrecen/István út

Eger/Lenin út

Gyöngyös/Szoloskert

Györ/Tompa U.

Miskolc/Pesti #2

Pěcs, Furst S. u.

Siófok/Hwy 70

Sopron, Kofarago tér

Szeged/Uttoro tér

Szekszárd/Hwy 56

Szentendre

Szombathely/Zanti út

Tata, MI Motorway

Zalaegerszeg/Balaton 2

This is a partial listing. Be sure to buy your gas before 6:00 p.m. For a complete listing, consult the *Travel Hungary* booklet available from the Hungary Tourist Promotion Board at H-1149 Budapest Angol #22 (tel. 163-3652, ext. 381 or 383). You can pick one up at Tourinform, #2 Suto út in Budapest. Tel. 117-9800. A complete map of all unleaded stations in Eastern Europe is available from any ADAC auto club office in Germany.

MONEY

On arrival, buy some forints. For a rough conversion of dollars to forints, multiply the forint amount by 1.4 and move the decimal point over two places to the left. For example, 720 forints are worth about $10. Money is easily exchanged at banks, hotels, and Ibusz and other tourist offices throughout Hungary.

TELEPHONE

As with all calls from the United States, you must first dial 011 for international long distance, then 36 for the Hungarian country code followed by the local city code and number. City codes relevant to Hungarian cities in this book are Budapest (1), Szentendre and Visegrád (26), Esztergom (33), Sopron (99), Köszeg (94), and Eger (36). Thus, to reach 436/7432 in Budapest, you would dial 011-36-1-436/7432. To phone the United States from Hungary, use USA Direct by calling 0036-0111. More information on this service can be found in the introduction. Local calls to smaller towns can take a long time to complete. Try your call during off-peak hours.

Budapest

This city of two million is a perfect gateway to one of Eastern Europe's fastest changing countries. Because it has the most advanced economy of the Eastern European nations, many Western businesses have set up bases here. The city is bustling with entrepreneurs who believe Budapest is the place to cut deals that will tap the market that is emerging from behind the Iron Curtain. While there is much talk of joint ventures aimed at developing manufacturing and industry, there is no doubt that Budapest's biggest enterprise is the city itself. Hundreds of new travel companies have opened in the past two years, and tourists have become the nation's leading source of badly needed foreign exchange.

Probably the only city in the world to operate an around-the-clock tourist information office that can arrange your accommodations, Budapest is easy to visit and enjoy. Because it is an affordable city, you can live comfortably here and take advantage of some remarkable restaurants, shops, and theaters. An excellent transit system, splendid museums and monuments, plenty of good restaurants, and a wide range of places to stay in all price categories make it a smart choice. One of the best features of the Hungarian capital is its proximity to picturesque villages, rural monasteries, cathedrals, and castles. Many of them are easy day trips. Depending on your mood, spend your days biking Danube islands or marveling at treasures like a splendid collection of late Gothic winged altarpieces.

Art and architecture are two of the city's claims to fame. At Aquincum, you can see portions of the first Roman town built here a century before Christ. In the ninth century, Hungarian tribes from the east created this state. When the Turks invaded in the sixteenth century, many Hungarians were taken into slavery. In 1636, when the Turks were vanquished, the Hapsburgs arrived from Austria and began their imperial reign that lasted more than two centuries. The Gothic and Romanesque landmarks that survived the Turkish onslaught were soon complemented by landmarks created by the baroque masters.

By the nineteenth century, Buda and Pest, two settlements facing each other across the Danube, had become the nation's hub. In 1872, they merged with the town of Óbuda and became Budapest. The late nineteenth century was the heyday of the Grunderzeit architecture that gave the city many neo-Renaissance landmarks. This eclectic style culminated at the end of the century with the creation of Andrássy Street, a grand boulevard built for the 1,000-year celebration commemorating the arrival of the Magyars. This monumental project took fourteen years to complete.

Today the center remains true to its architectural heritage, and there are only a few modern buildings in the hotel districts along the Danube. Even some of these, such as the Hilton on the Buda side, have been built to enhance the city's castle district. A veritable trans-

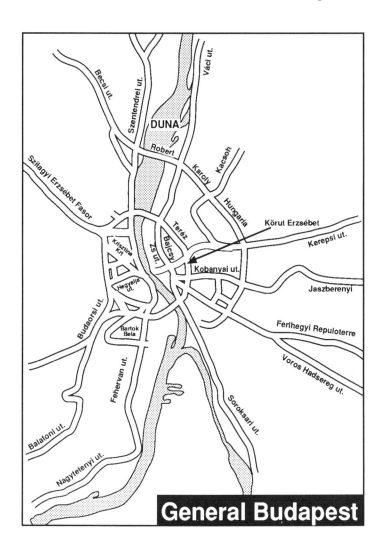

General Budapest

portation museum, the city is easily traveled via tram, funicular, subway, bus, bicycle, and, of course, by foot. Part of the fun is to see some of the none-too-subtle signs of liberation. More than a hundred street names associated with the Communist era have reverted to their original designations. On boulevards, banners announce the arrival of two men of letters, George Orwell (for his play, *1984*) and Hugh M. Hefner for the Hungarian translation of his hedonistic magazine.

As you explore Budapest, take time to visit some of the city's byways as well as its famous attractions. Step down a quiet side street and you may find a shop selling colorful Hungarian postage stamps, a special gelato, or folk art. Even some of the city's office buildings are worth a visit to marvel at the nonstop lifts that function like elevators without doors. Hop on or off at the right moment or you are likely to be injured.

While Budapest is a city of great physical beauty, do not overlook its siren sounds. From the ubiquitous Gypsy and Hungarian folk groups to jazz clubs to symphony orchestras, this city offers a remarkable variety of venues. Even the subway stations have informal trios entertaining passing travelers. Don't be surprised if you find yourself humming a few bars as you go about your daily rounds, enjoying a city that knows how to have a good time.

GETTING AROUND

Budapest has three metro lines operating between 4:30 a.m. and 11:00 p.m. Trams/streetcars, buses, and trolley buses run from 4:30 a.m. to 11:00 p.m., but some trams operate 24 hours. Purchase tickets at metro stations or tobacco shops (*Dohany bolt*) before boarding. The yellow ticket is valid for trams, trolley buses, and the metro. For the bus you need a blue ticket. Both cost 12 to 15 forints. Day and month passes (you need a photo for the latter) are also available. Tickets need to be validated by a device on the vehicle or at the entrance of the metro.

LODGING

Ibusz, the Hungarian travel company, operates, as far as we know, the only 24-hour tourist booking office in Europe. Here you can get information, change money, and, most important, book accom-

Fisherman's Bastion, Budapest, Hungary

modations ranging from a $10-a-night homestay to an unhosted apartment starting at $40 a night. We think this is the best deal in town for the midrange or budget traveler. If you stay in a hosted apartment, try to find a host that speaks some English. This office can also help arrange hotel accommodations as well as car rentals, rail, boat, and air tickets, and tours in Budapest or other parts of Hungary. If you are traveling in the busy summer season or during a holiday, it's easy to call or fax ahead to line up a place to stay (tel. 118-4864 or 118-4865; fax 117-9099). Your travel agent can book Hungarian hotel rooms (but not private accommodations) through Ibusz in Fort Lee, New Jersey, by calling (800) 367-1878.

If you are torn between staying on the Buda side or the Pest side, why not settle for Margaret Island in the Danube? A quiet spot that is convenient to both parts of town, it is the home of the luxurious **Ramada Grand Hotel**. While this historic hotel has lost some of its charm to an architectural makeover, it's still an inviting place to stay. You'll enjoy the thermal baths. Rooms start at about 8,640 forints ($120). Tel. 132-1100; fax 153-3029; or call (800) 228-9898 in the United States. Next door is the **Thermal Hotel Margaret Island**, a more contemporary structure offering rooms in the same price range. Tel. 132-1100; fax 153-3029.

On the Buda side, the **Hilton Hotel** at Hess A. tér #1-3 offers beautiful views of the city. Rooms here also run about 8,640 forints ($120). Tel. 175-1000; fax 156-0285. The **Atrium Hyatt Hotel** located on the Pest side at #2 Roosevelt tér is convenient to the business center, Parliament, and Váci utca, the city's prime shopping district. Tel. 138-3000; fax 117-9788. Rooms here start at 13,320 forints (about $185). The nearby **Hotel Forum** at #12-14 Apáczai Csere runs about 9,720 forints ($135). Tel. 117-8088; fax 117-9808.

In the moderate price range is the **Gellért** at #1 Szt Gellért tér on the Buda side. Famous for its baths and pools, it offers a grand view of the Danube and is only five minutes from either the castle or the Pest commercial center. Tel. 185-2200; fax 166-6631. Rooms start around 5,760 forints ($80). In the same price range is the **Hotel Béke Radisson**, #43 Teréz krt. It is close to the Nyugati Railway Station and the metro, which can take you to the Pest center in just ten minutes. The **Flamenco Occidental** at #7 Tas vezér runs about

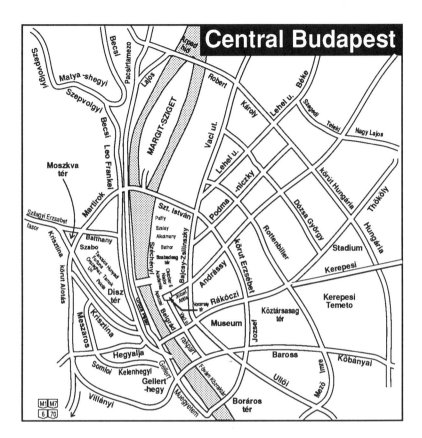

5,040 forints ($70). It is on the Buda side about 10 minutes by bus from the castle or the Pest commercial district. Tel. 161-2250; fax 165-8007.

The **Hotel Erzsébet** in the center of Pest near the Elizabeth Bridge, at #11-15 Karolyi M. Ult, offers rooms for about 3,500 forints ($50). Tel. 227-494. In the same price range is the **Liget** at #106 Dózsa Gy. utca. This hotel has an attractive location near the City Park and the fine arts museum. It is about 20 minutes by bus from the heart of Pest. Tel. 111-3200. The **Hotel Normafa**, complete with pool and massage services, is located at #52-54 Normafa

On the road to Vajdahunyad Castle, Budapest, Hungary

utca. It is near the Buda Castle, and about 15 minutes by foot and funicular to the Pest side. Tel. 156-3444.

If you would prefer staying in a youth hostel, book ahead by writing to **Expressz Kozponti Iroda**, #4 Semmelweis utca, Budapest V. Tel. 117-6634. Units run about 210 to 720 forints ($3 to $10) per night. Or visit the hostel office, which is open from 8:00 a.m. to 5:00 p.m. Monday through Thursday and 8:00 a.m. to 4:30 p.m. on Friday. For a list of campsites in the Budapest area, write to **Tourinform** at 1052 Budapest, #2 Suto utca, or call 117-9800 to request their listing of locations across the country.

If you are interested in saving money, consider a homestay arranged through the Ibusz 24-hour office mentioned above. You can request an English-speaking host—a great way to get to know a local family. Renting an unhosted apartment through Ibusz at 2,885 forints ($40) is also a good deal for groups. Many apartments come with kitchen facilities and are well located.

FOOD

For an elegant splurge, consider **Garvices** at #2 Urömi köz in Óbuda (Old Buda). Barbecued and roasted dishes are specialties on a menu that includes international and Hungarian cuisine. Closed Sunday. Tel. 168-3254. **Barokk** at #12 Mozsar utca near the Operetta Theater is a good choice for traditional Hungarian food, baroque music, and period ambience. Tel. 131-8942. In the castle area on the Buda side, try **Alabárdos** at #2 Országhaz utca. Tel. 156-0851. Another possibility is **Gundel** at #2 Állatkerti út in the City Park area. Tel. 122-0021.

Moderately priced restaurants include the **Café New York** at #9 Erzsébet krt. The fantastic baroque interior makes this one of Eastern Europe's authentic landmarks. Tel. 122-3849. Also worth visiting is **Karpatia** at #1 Ferencesek tér. Tel. 117-3596.

One of the best budget restaurants in town is **Bohémtanya** at #6 Paulay Ede near the Deak tér metro stop. This unpretentious spot offers excellent food, huge portions, and menus in three languages. Tel. 122-1453. The *palascintas* are terrific. **Adám** at #41 Andrássy út is famous for the best beef tartar in town. Tel. 122-4620. **Alföldi** at #3 Kecskemetí utca specializes in dishes from the Great Plain area. Tel. 117-4404.

Cafés

Gerbeaud Confectionary at #7 Vörösmarty tér is a fine place to relax in the heart of Pest. Tel. 118-1311. Another good possibility is Müvész Confectionary at #29 Andrássy út. Tel. 122-4606. Café Pierrot at #14 Fortuna utca is a privately owned piano bar in the castle area. It is open from 5:00 p.m. to 1:00 a.m. Monday through Saturday and 11:00 a.m. to 11:00 p.m. Sunday. Tel. 175-6971.

NIGHTLIFE

The Merlin Jazz Club Restaurant at #4 Gerlóczy utca offers two sets nightly at 8:00 and 10:00 as well as midnight shows on Friday and Saturday. Tel. 117-9338. Rock Café at #20 Dohány utca has live music, mostly rock with some blues, Latin, and jazz from 6:00 p.m. to 3:00 a.m. Paradiso disco bar is located in a private villa at #40/1 Istenhegyi. It is open from 10:00 p.m. to 6:00 a.m. There is also an expensive restaurant here which is open from noon until midnight. Orfeum in the Hotel Béke Radisson at #43 Teréz krt. has an evening program beginning at 10:45.

OPERA AND CLASSICAL MUSIC

The Hungarian State Opera at #22 Andrássy út performs regularly at 7:00 p.m. and offers selected special performances at 11:00 a.m. Tickets can be purchased from the Central Theater Booking office at #18 Andrássy út (tel. 112-0000) or in Buda at #3 Moszkva tér (tel. 135-9136). Tickets are also available at the opera house itself. They are extremely reasonable, only a few dollars.

A wide variety of performances are offered at the Vigadó concert hall on Vigadó tér around the corner from Vorosmarty tér. This splendid hall, which is reached via a grand staircase, should not be missed. Make it a point to enjoy a concert or recital here (tel. 117-6222, ext. 110).

SPAS AND BATHS

Gellért in the Hotel Gellért (see Lodging, above) offers thermal baths Monday through Friday from 6:30 a.m. to 7:00 p.m., Saturday 6:30 a.m. to 1:00 p.m., and Sunday 6:30 a.m. to noon. The swimming pool is open daily from 6:00 a.m. to 6:00 p.m. In the City Park, **Széchenyi's** thermal baths are open Monday through Friday from 6:30 a.m. to 7 p.m., Saturday 6:30 a.m. to 1:00 p.m., and Sunday from 6:30 a.m. to noon. The swimming pool is open Monday through Sunday from 6:00 a.m. to 6:00 p.m. Tel. 121-0310. **Rudas** at #9 Döbrentei tér is open Monday through Friday from 6:00 a.m. to 7:00 p.m., Saturday from 6:00 a.m. to 1:00 p.m., and Sunday 6:00 a.m. to noon. Because there are different days for men and women, call before you go. Tel. 175-4449.

SHOPPING

For bargains on handmade toys, try **Burattino Jatekbolt**, #57 Kazinczy út. Communist artifacts are found in **The Last Breath of Communism Kiosk** at the entrance to Vajdahunyad Castle, City Park. Choose from Lenin pins, Communist apparel, rubles, red stars, and collectibles from the Iron Curtain era at bargain basement prices. For furniture, textiles, leather, ceramics, and metal work and other arts and crafts, head for **Kezmuves**, #16 Timar út. **Egyetemi Könyvesbolt** at #18 Kossuth Lajos specializes in books for tourists (tel. 118-3318). Also try **Corvina** at #6 Kossuth Lajos. **Folkart Centrum**, #14 Váci út, is the place to find puppets, embroidery, pottery, and leather (tel. 118-5840). **Filatelia** at #17-19 Petofi Sandor út has an outstanding collection of commemoratives and sets (tel. 118-5101).

HELPFUL HINTS

Tourist information, including accommodations, tours and tickets, is available at **Tourinform**, #2 Sütö utca, just 50 meters from the Deák tér metro station. The office is open every day from 8:00 a.m. to 8:00 p.m. Tel. 117-9800. Museums are generally open Tuesday through Sunday from 10:00 a.m. to 6:00 p.m. We indicate when Budapest museums operate on other schedules. It is always a good idea to phone ahead and double check hours as they are subject to change.

SIGHTSEEING

The Castle District

The best place to begin your visit to Budapest is Clark Adam tér on the Buda side where you board the cable car to Castle Hill. Easily reached on foot from the Pest side via the Chain (Lánchid) Bridge, this swift system operates from 8:30 a.m. to 10:00 p.m. daily. You will alight in the midst of the Castle District and enjoy an excellent overview of the entire city. Take some time to stroll along the castle terraces or ascend the turreted **Fisherman's Bastion** built at the turn of the century to commemorate the 1,000th anniversary of Hungary's founding. During the Middle Ages, a fish market operated at the site of this fanciful white stone landmark. The Fishermen's Guild fought to defend this section of the wall. From here you can spot a few of the destinations you are likely to see over the next few days. On your far left is Margaret Island, a must for any visitor. Continuing south along the Danube you will be able to spot the neo-Gothic Parliament. Also easy to see are St. Stephen's Basilica and, in the distance, Vajdahunyad Castle, a Hungarian/Transylvanian hybrid.

One of the unique features of the Castle District is that it invites exploration above- and belowground as well as at street level. Because most cars have been banned from the area, it is possible to undertake a leisurely exploration of the Buda byways here on Castle Hill. After visiting the fourteenth-century **Matthias Church** on Szentháromság tér, head west on Szentháromság út to Toth Arpad setany, and turn right (north) to the **Military History Museum** at #43. Tel. 156-9522. It is open Tuesday through Saturday from 9:00 a.m. to 5:00 p.m., Sunday and holidays 10:00 a.m. to 6:00 p.m. Also worth a visit are the antique instruments and Béla Bartók collections at the **Music History Museum/Hungarian Academy of Sciences**, #7 Tansics M. utca. Hours are Monday from 4:00 p.m. to 9:00 p.m. and Wednesday through Sunday from 10:00 a.m. to 6:00 p.m. Tel. 156-6858. Beethoven really did sleep here. Be sure not to miss the Béla Pinter-designed **Hilton** at #1-3 Hess A tér. This may be the only hotel in the world built around the Gothic remains of a Dominican church. A former Jesuit cloister wall is also part of the intriguing Hilton building.

Royal Palace, Budapest, Hungary

From the Matthias Church, take Szentháromság utca west one block to Uri út and proceed south to #9. Here you will find the entrance to the Buda Castle Labyrinth, where tour guides take you through the limestone catacombs. It is open daily from 10:00 a.m. to 6:00 p.m. Call 175-7533 to confirm hours in the off-season. After exploring the Buda underground, which served as a bomb shelter during World War II, continue south to the **Royal Palace** and the city's largest museum complex. Of the many fine collections in Eastern Europe, this is one of the best. Art, architecture, religion, history, and politics are conveniently showcased here in a majestic setting. A few well-spent hours will add immeasurably to your appreciation and enjoyment of the fascinating culture of Hungary and its neighbors.

Returning south past the cable car depot, you'll head through neo-baroque gates to the castle complex. Directly in front of you is the **Royal Palace**, Hungary's ultimate home remodeling project. The original Gothic structure was demolished by the Christian armed forces that freed this city from the Turks in the late seventeenth century. Completely rebuilt and expanded during the following century, the landmark was ornamented with art nouveau touches. Badly damaged during World War II, the castle received a postwar face lift that included a new baroque facade.

Today the castle is the home of three outstanding Budapest Museums. First visit the **National Gallery**, best known for its panoramic collection of Hungarian painting and sculpture, located in Wings C and D. It is open Tuesday through Sunday. From early July through early November, hours are 10:00 a.m. to 6:00 p.m. Stone relics and panel paintings from the Middle Ages as well as Renaissance and baroque art are exhibited here. My favorite room is the collection of late Gothic **winged altarpieces**, immaculately restored in a Romanesque setting. Collected from churches around the nation, these triptychs are a high point of Eastern European religious art. Particularly notable is the fifteenth-century altar from St. John the Baptist Church in Kissebahn.

In addition to the National Gallery be sure to visit the **Modern History Museum** in Wing A. It replaced the Communists' Museum of the Working Class Movement. Dedicated to the revolution that brought democracy to this land in 1989, this is a good place to learn the story of the historic transformation. In addition to permanent exhibits, special exhibits focus on subjects like news photography and world politics. Be sure not to overlook the third castle collection at the **Budapest Historical Museum** in Wing E (tel. 175-7533). The permanent exhibit offers an archaeological time line of this 2,000-year-old city. Much of the museum focuses on the evolution of this eclectic castle. Patient excavation has recovered many important treasures from the city's past including remnants of the old St. George Square, portions of the original palace, pillars from the dry moat, and the first gate and tower. The art history of the castle is beautifully presented. Also here are treasures from the past like King Matthias's fifteenth-century tableware and a fascinating photographic retrospective on the past century of Budapest architecture.

Beautiful Downtown Pest

The city's leading promenade, Váci Street, leads to Budapest's hub, **Vörösmarty tér**, named for a nineteenth-century poet. Street musicians and performers, hurried business people, students, families, and tourists like yourself make this a great place to begin your visit to Pest's inner city. Enjoy a ringside seat at the elegant **Gerbeaud** café, a nineteenth-century classic known for its fine pastries. Within minutes you can reach many of the city's most attractive venues. But the square itself is a good place to spend some time resting up for the sightseeing in the Belvaros district.

A very pleasant walk leads south through the inner city on **Váci utca**, Budapest's leading shopping street. Along the way you'll pass the Philanthia flower shop, an art nouveau classic at #9, and the postmodern Taverna Hotel, at #20. At Pesti Barnabas, turn right to the Danube embankment. Continue north past major hotels and a number of tempting sidewalk cafés and restaurants until you reach Bathori út. Then go left in front of the baroque/Gothic parliament building ornamented with more than 230 statues. This, the largest public building in Budapest, is an enduring monument to the political process. Historian Katalin Pallai writes in *My Hungary* that "shortly after Parliament was opened in 1904 two dozen policemen were forced to clear the building of. . . representatives of the oppo-

Statue of Anonymous in Városliget Park, Budapest, Hungary

sition...after they had smashed the furnishings owing to a disagreement on political issues."
    In front of the parliament at #12 Kossuth Lajos tér is the **Ethnographic Museum**. Do not miss this collection of Hungarian folk art, historical artifacts, crafts, and culture. Also here are exhibits on Eskimos, African music, and masks from Melanesia. Tel. 132-6340. Return to Bathori út and continue east to Bajcsy-Zellinszky út. Go south (right) to **St. Stephen's Church**. This nineteenth-century neo-Renaissance cathedral, crowned by a basilica that is nearly 300 feet high, is the largest church in Budapest, with room for more than 8,000 worshipers. It honors the church's patron saint and is home to the most important reliquary object in Hungarian Catholicism, St. Stephen's right hand.

Andrássy Street to City Park

Beginning at Bajcsy-Zsilinszky út and Erzsébet tér, Andrássy is an architectural showcase and the best route to City Park. By foot (about an hour), cab, car, or bus, this fin-de-siècle street has many landmarks such as the **Hungarian State Opera House** at #22 Andrássy út. It took nine years to complete the vision of architect Miklós Ybl. The opera house is adorned with the statues of famed Hungarian composers like Ferenc Liszt and illuminated by three-ton bronze chandeliers. Half a dozen of the nation's leading artists decorated the interior. For a few dollars you can attend an opera here, one of Eastern Europe's great musical bargains. Tickets are available at the opera house and the Central Theater Booking Office, #18 Andrássy út (tel. 112-0000), or at their Buda office, #3 Moszkva tér (tel. 135-9136). Most performances begin at 7:00 p.m. There are also occasional performances at 11:00 a.m.
    After pausing for coffee and pastry at Müvész Confectionary at #29 Andrássy or Lukács Confectioner at #70 Andrássy, continue to Hero's Square, site of the **Millennial Monument**. Built to honor the anniversary of Hungary's settlement, this colonnaded landmark has been altered over the years. Following World War II, memorials then dedicated to the Hapsburgs were replaced by Hungarian freedom fighters who led the Magyar tribes. Statues also honor Hungary's first king, St. Stephen, and numerous other members of royalty.

Adjacent to the square is the **Museum of Fine Arts** at #41 Dozsa Gyorgy út (tel. 142-9759). This collection showcases Hungarian artists as well as Greek statues, Spanish masters, English landscapes, modern sculpture, and paintings by Gauguin, Renoir, Cézanne, and Toulouse-Lautrec. Next to the museum is **Gundel** at #2 Állatkerti utca. Tel. 122-1002. One of the city's more elegant restaurants, this is a popular spot for banquets. In warm weather, the patio is a delight. Gundel is located in **City Park** (Vársoliget), home of Budapest's zoo, circus, and amusement park. Also here is **Széchenyi Baths** at #11 Állatkerti körút. Tel. 121-0310. With more than two million visitors annually, this is one of the most popular thermal pools in Europe. Chess buffs will appreciate the floating boards that make it easy to play while taking the waters.

City Park is also the home of **Vajdahunyad Castle**, which looks like an antecedent of Disneyland's Fantasyland castle. Gothic, Romanesque, and baroque architecture make this turreted building a Budapest landmark. Beautifully illuminated at night, this is the perfect setting for a Halloween party. Also here in the castle area are the **Museum of Agriculture** and the **Museum of Natural Sciences**.

Elsewhere in Budapest

Nagykörút, Budapest's Great Boulevard, is a loop that extends from the Margaret Bridge to the Petofi Bridge on the Pest side. While the street name changes from Szt István körút to Teréz to Erzsébet to Jozsef to Ferenc, the boulevard is continuous. Construction began in 1872 and took 35 years to complete. Designed to link up five different neighborhoods, this thoroughfare is one you'll see many times during your visit. The **Western Railway Station** at #55 Teréz körút was built while the Great Boulevard was under construction. This cast iron building with a glass facade is one of the city's architectural landmarks. Another is the neo-Renaissance **Café New York** at #9-11 Erzsébet körút, a mandatory stop for any Budapest visitor. Early in this century, it became a favorite gathering place for the Hungarian intelligentsia. Their caricatures of one another still hang from the restaurant walls. The eclectic interior makes you feel like you are dining in a palace.

July 2, 1916

Cavendish, PEI

It has been fun to "tour around" "Anne" sights here in PEI. House of Green Gables up to expectations and the Lovers Lane and Balsam Hollow Haunted Woods nearby were just as one might imagine. We went to a special evening program at Green Gables featuring a walk with Lucy Maud Montgomery through the woods & ending with Anne Shirley convincing Marilla to invite us into Green Gables for cookies! The north shore of PEI is beautiful - red cliffs, beaches, dunes, etc. Ann, Stephen, Peter & Elizabeth

Jennie Levine
10004 Whitworth Way
Ellicott City, MD 21043
USA

52
Canada

Gravenstein Apple
Pomme de Gravenstein

Green Gables

A short walk west of the Great Boulevard at #14-16 Muzeum körút is the **National Museum** (tel. 138-2122), Hungary's largest. It is best known for its display of the Crown Jewels. The Hungarian Crown, entrusted to the American army at the end of World War II, was returned to Budapest by the U.S. government in 1978. Also of special interest are the orb, which represented each Hungarian king on the crown mantle, and the sword, made in Venice in the early sixteenth century. Important collections here focus on Hungarian archaeology, medieval history, and historical portraits.

Continue north on Muzeum krt. to Dohany utca and turn right. At #2-8 Dohany út is one of Europe's largest synagogues. Now the **National Jewish Museum**, it is generally open from 10:00 a.m. to 1:00 p.m. weekdays, but hours are subject to change. Hungarian-Jewish expatriates have raised funds to help restore this Byzantine-Moorish landmark that has room for a congregation of 3,000. Among those who have played the organ here is Saint-Saens. **Theodore Herzl**, the founder of modern Zionism, was born next door. Directly behind the museum is a sculpture memorial to Jewish victims of the Holocaust. Many were shot in cold blood by Nazi troops who stormed the ghetto district in the nightmare autumn of 1944. Others perished on horrifying death marches to the concentration camps or in the camps themselves. Actor Tony Curtis, the son of Hungarian Jewish immigrants, helped raise the funds for this memorial. Another important memorial on the Buda side of town honors **Raoul Wallenberg**, the onetime Swedish playboy who led an underground campaign that saved thousands of Hungarian Jews from the gas chamber in 1944. Take the metro to Moszkva tér and pick up a #56 tram or bus west on Szilagyi Erzsébet. The memorial is located a few minutes beyond the Hotel Budapest. Wallenberg was arrested for espionage by the Soviets after the war; his disappearance is one of the great mysteries of the Cold War era.

After paying your respects here, you may want to head down to the Danube embankment and pick up a bus to **Margaret Island**. Reached via the Margaret Bridge (bus #26 or 26A from the Pest side or #4 or 6 from Moszkva tér on the Buda side), this is a wonderful car-free environment. Inhabited as far back as Roman times, it became a church state in the thirteenth century. After the Mongols defeated the Hungarian Royal Army, King Bela IV promised to send his daughter Margaret off to a rural convent if he could save the nation. When the Mongols retreated, the king built a convent here and Margaret lived on the island for the rest of her life. It is named in her memory. You can rent a bike, take the waters at the Thermal Hotel or Ramada Grand, swim outdoors in the Palatinus pool, explore the rose or Japanese gardens, and photograph Buda and Pest from an excellent vantage point. Theater, ballet, and opera are performed outdoors here in the summer months.

The Danube Bend

The Danube extends from the Black Forest to the Black Sea, flowing 1,770 miles across Germany, Czechoslovakia, Austria, Hungary, Romania, and Bulgaria. About 240 miles of this river cross Hungary, and some of the best scenery is found along the Danube Bend, a region that begins just north of Budapest. Three principal towns, Szentendre, Visegrád, and Esztergom, are the main destinations for visitors. But the entire region north of Budapest is a gem. You will find Roman forts, historic castles, religious museums, and some of the nation's most innovative architecture. For a day trip or a week-long visit, this region is one of Hungary's star attractions.

The place to start is **Aquincum** overlooking the Danube's west bank in the Óbuda district on Budapest's north end. These ruins, easily reached via the HEV train from the terminal at Batthyany tér (disembark at the Aquincum station), are on the road to Szentendre. The second-century amphitheater, Hercules villa, Roman baths, and chapel remains were discovered in the late 1930s during a construction project. The Romans were ultimately vanquished by the barbarians, including Attila the Hun who allegedly lived here in the fifth century. The area was later taken by the Magyars, and Aquincum became part of Óbuda, one of the three cities that ultimately

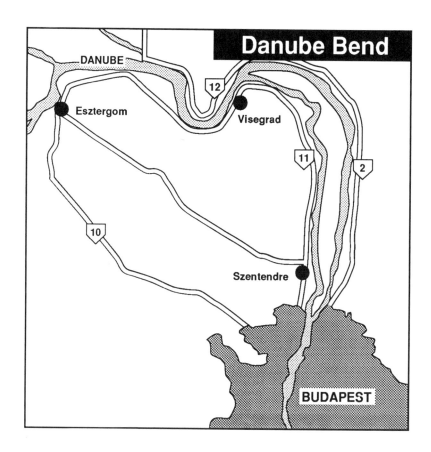

became merged into Budapest. Many important artifacts are exhibited at the Táborvárosi Museum and the Aquincum Museum, #139 Szentendre út. A major campground, Romani, is located about half a mile north of Aquincum on the Danube bank. Also here is a major outdoor pool. Both are convenient to the HEV rail station.

GETTING THERE

Easily reached by boat, public transit, or rental car, the Danube Bend is a must for any visitor to Budapest. If you have the time, why not consider an overnight excursion to enjoy its many pleasures? If your time is limited, you may want to simply head down to Vigadó

Capitalist vegetable stand, Budapest, Hungary

tér and board the morning ferry. It takes about 45 minutes to reach
Szentendre, three hours to Visegrád, and five hours to Esztergom.
Boats depart at 7:00 a.m., 7:30 a.m., and 2:00 p.m. from the end of
April until late September. They arrive in Visegrád at 10:20 a.m.,
10:35 a.m., and 5:00 p.m. Arrival in Esztergom is at 12:10 p.m.,
12:40 p.m., and 7:00 p.m. Boats return from Esztergom at 8:30 a.m.,
3:30 p.m., and 4:30 p.m. Summer hydrofoil service departs
Budapest on Friday, Saturday, and Sunday at 9:00 a.m., arriving in
Esztergom at 10:30 a.m. Return service departs at 5:00 p.m., arriving back in Budapest at 6:30 p.m.

The 7:30 a.m. boat from Budapest stops in Szentendre at 9:05
a.m. During the peak summer season, boats make the one hour and
50 minute trip from Budapest to Szentendre at 8:30 a.m., 10:00
a.m., 2:00 p.m., and 3:00 p.m. (There is more limited boat service
in the off-season). You can make a round-trip by boat or return by
bus or train. A car will add considerable flexibility to your itinerary.

In the heart of the Pest district, Budapest, Hungary

If your time is limited, hop the HEV train that departs Budapest's Batthyány tér station every fifteen to thirty minutes for the 12-mile trip to Szentendre.

Szentendre

While its roots are Roman, the heart of this charming town was created by the Serbians, Greeks, and Dalmatians. Szentendre has more than a dozen museums, beautiful churches, fine shops, galleries, and restaurants and is an ideal place to spend a morning or afternoon. Exploring its cobblestone streets or Danube embankment is like stepping back in time. Szentendre is especially pleasant in the early evening hours when much of the town turns out to enjoy life on the waterfront.

There are many inviting places to stay in Szentendre, a town within commuting distance of Budapest. Its pleasant riverfront setting and relative tranquillity make it a great way to escape the city's

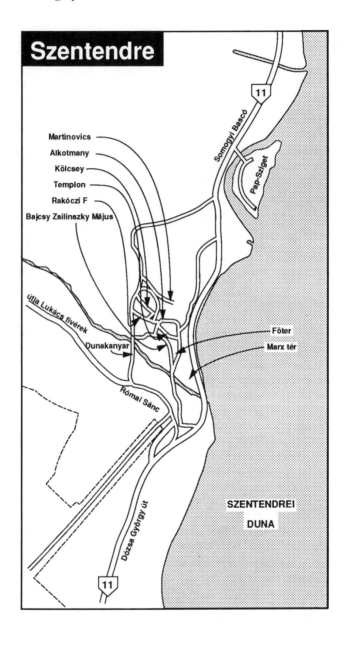

noise and traffic. For homestay information, check with the town tourist office located just off Fö tér at #1 Bogdanyi utca (tel. 26/10315). Dunatours (tel. 26/11311) can also help you find accommodations. Many families also advertise their own rooms. Look for the Zimmer Frei sign. If you prefer a hotel, consider the **Danubius** at #28 Ady Endre út where doubles run 2,073 forints ($28). Tel. 26/12511. A room at the **Coca-Cola Guest-House** at #50 Dunakanyar körút is $34.80. Tel. 26/10410. The **Hubertus Pension** at #10 Tyukos dulö charges 2,376 forints ($33). Tel. 26/10616. The budget **Hotel Fenyves** at #26 Ady Endre út runs 620 forints ($10). Tel. 26/11882. Hostel-type dorm accommodations are available at the **Köhegyi Turistaház**, #16 Köhegyi. Tel. 26/12292. You can also take a bus north of town to campground resorts on Szentendre Island, which extends 18 miles from northern Budapest to Visegrád. To reach the **Ságvári Endre Tourist Hostel**, take a local bus three miles to Lajos-forrás. **Aquatours Camping** is at #9-11 Ady E. út. Tel. 26/11106. About four miles north of Szentendre on Route 11 is **Leányfalu**, a popular camping resort. Tel. 26/23154.

Szentendre also has a number of restaurants worth trying. They include **Aranysárkány étterem** at #1/a Alkotmany út (tel. 26/11670); **Rab Ráby étterem**, #1 Peter Pal út (tel. 26/10819); **Régimódi étterem** at #2 Dumtsa Jeno út (tel. 26/11105); and **Serfözde a varoshazahoz** (tel. 26/12700).

Szentendre looks more Mediterranean than Eastern European —the kind of town you would expect to find in Yugoslavia's Dalmatia. A good place to begin your journey through Szentendre is the **Open-Air Ethnographic Museum**. This collection preserves eighteenth- and nineteenth-century life-styles (it's 2 miles northwest of town and easily reached by bus from the Szentendre rail station). Historic houses, stables, an old mill, a blacksmith's shop, a baker's oven, and a graveyard re-create the town's past. It is open from April through October, Tuesday through Sunday from 9:00 a.m. to 5:00 p.m. Tel. 26/12304. The town is also a popular artist's colony with more than a dozen galleries and is therefore a good place to shop for contemporary art. Some of the best is exhibited at the **Szentendre Keptar**, #2-5 Fö tér. Also worth a visit is the the art collection at **Amos Imre-Anna Margit Museum** at #10 Bogdanyi út. Paintings here range from biblical to antiwar themes. The **Margit**

Szentendre, Hungary (Courtesy Ibusz, Hungarian Travel Company)

Kovács Museum located in an eighteenth-century house at #1 Vastagh György utca honors the life of one of Hungary's best-known twentieth-century artists. Tel. 26/10244. Nearby is the **Ferenczy Museum** at #6 Fö tér, featuring the work of Hungarian impressionist Károly Ferenczy and his children.

Religious art flourishes in Szentendre, a town famous for its Catholic, Serbian Orthodox, and Calvinist churches. The baroque **Blagovestenska Church** on Fö tér is a Hungarian landmark. Nearby, is the **Belgrade Church** at Alkotmany út and Fö tér where you will want to see the remarkable marble altar with a rococo pulpit. Behind this church at #5 Engels út is the **Serbian Collection of Ecclesiastical Art**, famous for its icons including a Greek panel painting of the Nativity and the Kazan Virgin from the Soviet Union. Also well worth a visit is the **Museum of Roman Stonework Finds** at #7 Római sànc utca.

Visegrád

Located fourteen miles north of Szentendre, this small town lives securely in the past. Considering its estimable history, that is hardly a surprise. In the mid-thirteenth century, the royal family began work on a castle that evolved into a 350-room Gothic-Renaissance palace. Italian Renaissance sculptors, architects, and masons created a home fit for a king. Early in the fourteenth century, the Anjous moved the royal seat here, and Visegrád became one of the most opulent royal residences in Europe. At grand feasts red and white wine poured out of the Renaissance garden's Courtyard of the Lion fountain.

After the Turks took control of Hungary in the mid-sixteenth century, the castle was abandoned and ultimately buried by a series of landslides. Excavation began in 1934, and today the **castle ruins** make this Danube hillside one of Hungary's great archaeological treasures. While the dig continues, you can see remains of the great marble fountain, Gothic cloisters, and the chapel, baths, and wall painting remnants. The **Citadel** and the nearby **Silvanus Hotel** are great places to enjoy a view of the Bend. While here, visit the Visegrád excursion center at **Pills Park Forest** designed by famed Hungarian architect Imre Makovecz. Of special interest is the reception building, which resembles a mill.

Esztergom

Esztergom was the home of Hungarian royalty until the arrival of the Mongols. And for more than 1,000 years, it has remained the seat of the nation's Catholic church. This is also a town where it is easy to rest up after several intense days of sightseeing in Budapest. Indeed, Esztergom, a town of 31,000, makes an excellent base for exploring the entire Bend region.

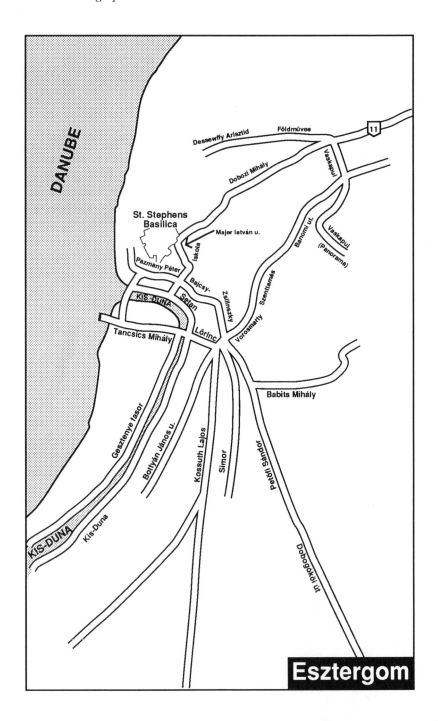

Sheepherding in Szirak, northern Hungary

If you are in an upscale mood, spend the night at the **Hotel Esztergom** located on the Kis-Danube canal at Primássziget, adjacent to the Danube. It is a short walk from the basilica. Rooms run about 7,200 forints ($60). Tel. 33/12883. Across the canal and less expensive is the **Hotel Volántourist** at #2 Jozsef A. tér. Rooms come with shared baths and run 864 forints ($12). Tel 33/12714. This is our recommended budget choice; some upper-story rooms have nice views of the canal. The **Ibusz** office is located at 2500 Martirok utca #1. Tel. 33/12552. **Komturist** is at #6 Martirok utca. Tel. 33/12082. There's camping at **Gran Camping Es Bungalow,** Nagy-Duna setany. Tel. 33/11327.

Recommended restaurants include **Fürdö étterem** at #14 Bajcsy Zsilinszky (tel. 33/11688); **Héviz étterem** (tel. 33/11688), Aradi vertanuk tér; **Kettös Pince étterem** at 2500 Banomi dulo (tel. 33/12224); and **Primás Pince Sötétkapu Sörözö** at 2500 Beke tér (tel. 33/13495).

Esztergom is best known for its **basilica** on Castle Hill which is the largest church in Hungary. Inside is the **Cathedral Treasury,**

Szirak, northern Hungary

one of the grandest ecclesiastical collections in Eastern Europe. Here you will see 1,000-year-old church vestments, artifacts, chalices, and crystal crosses. The cathedral library is Hungary's oldest, and local bishops rest in the basement crypt built in classic Egyptian style.

While the basilica is Esztergom's signature attraction, its crown jewel is the **Christian Museum**. It was founded nearly a century ago by the archbishop, Janos Simor, who spared no expense in his campaign to save irreplaceable Hungarian ecclesiastical art. In the process, Bishop Simor and his successors acquired many important treasures such as sixty-three early Italian panel paintings. The museum founders and their successors have been figures at religious art auctions around the continent, and their splendid acquisitions have created a collection that now attracts artists and art historians from all over the world. Among the highlights is a splendid exhibit of both Gothic and Renaissance triptychs, including the fifteenth-century Tamas of Kolozsvar winged altar. Hungarian, Austrian, German, Italian, and Flemish paintings include masterworks from the late Gothic, baroque, and Renaissance schools. Of special interest are the wood sculpture collection and French and Flemish tapestries.

Arguably the most important museum on the Danube Bend, this collection is a compelling reason for a visit to Esztergom.

Another good reason to visit is the town's beautiful riverfront setting. Take a walk up to the calvary chapel atop **St. Thomas Hill** for a panoramic look at the city and then head down to historic **Széchenyi Square** and the **Danube Museum** at #2 Kolcsey Ferenc út.

Eger

Just 72 miles northeast of Budapest, Eger can easily be reached by car, bus, or train in about two hours. This town of 64,000 is famous for its castle, architecture, religious and political history, thermal baths, and red wine. It is also the gateway to Hungary's picturesque Matra mountains, which reach a towering 3,000 feet. With its splendid town square, cathedral, fort, and Turkish minaret, Eger provides a convenient overview of the birth of a nation. It is also a lot of fun thanks to the fine resorts, hotels, restaurants, shops, and sightseeing opportunities that make this town a popular Hungarian getaway.

LODGING

The baths are close to the spacious **Hotel Flóra**, #5 Fürdö utca, which is about a ten-minute walk southeast of Dobó tér. Double rooms start at about 3,670 forints ($51). Tel. 36/20211; fax 36/20815. The **Eger Hotel** at #1-3 Szalloda utca runs 4,320 forints ($60). Tel. 36/13233. Slightly less expensive, about 1,800 to 2,500 forints ($25 to $35) a night, is the **Senator Ház**. It is at #11 Dobó tér. Tel. 36/20466; fax 36/13213. You can save money and meet the locals by booking at room in an apartment or home through **Ibusz**, Bajcsy Zsilinszky utca. Tel. 36/12526; fax 36/12652. A campground at #79 Rakoczi utca is served by buses #10 and #11. Tel. 36/10558. The **Esterházy Károly Tanárképzö Föiskola Lyceum** (youth hostel) is

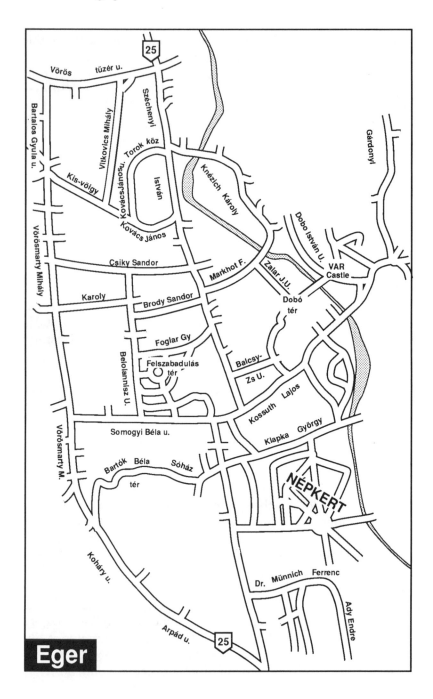

Eger

located at #1 Eszterházy tér. It is open from March 31 through the end of August. Tel. 36/10446; fax 36/10119. **Kastélyszálló Noszvaj** in Noszvaj is about ten minutes east of Eger. Tel. Noszvaj #2 (operator assisted). The castle, built in the late baroque style, makes guests feel like they are living in a museum.

FOOD

Restaurants worth trying are **Vörös Rák**, #11 Szent Janos (tel. 36/12814), and **Kazamata üzletház** on Martirok tér (tel. 36/13233). Eger is famous for its wine. A good place to try it is **Minorita Borozó**, a restaurant at #7/9 Dobó tér (tel. 36/20550). Another possibility from March through December is **Kulacs Csárda Borozó** (tel. 36/11375). It is located in Szépasszonyvolgy, a wooded area southwest of the city which is the heart of Eger's wine cellar district. This is one of over sixty cellars where you can sample famed local wines including the legendary **Bull's Blood of Eger**. Until the arrival of the Turks, this region was limited to white grapes. But Serbians fleeing from the advancing Turks brought red cuttings with them. Bull's Blood is a hybrid of such grapes as Kadarka, Grand Burgundy, Medoc noir, and Oporto. Although the vintages vary a little from year to year, the quality is excellent. The name behind the wine is attributed to Turks who got around Moslem blue laws by claiming the wine was actually bull's blood. Another explanation is that Eger defenders in the famous siege of 1552 fortified themselves with local red wine. The losing Turks, noticing the wine on their opponents lips, claimed that the bulls blood had turned their opponents into supermen.

SIGHTSEEING

Eger has nearly 200 significant monuments, so there is obviously a lot to do there. The good news is that much of the town can be seen on foot. While a day trip from Budapest will certainly suffice, many visitors use Eger as a base camp for their assault on the (3,000-foot-high) Matra mountains. Others prefer to concentrate on soaking up the hot springs. Whatever your pleasure, you can rest assured that Eger is sure to please.

Matthias Church, Budapest, Hungary

The best place to begin a visit is the heart of Eger on **Dobó Ist-ván tér**, the town's historic center. Site of the **Minorite Church**, a baroque landmark, this is one of Hungary's most colorful town squares. Enjoy it from the vantage point of a sidewalk café. From here it's only a few minutes to the town's best-known landmark, the **Eger Castle**. Begun in the thirteenth century, the castle took decades to complete. In 1552, a Turkish assault was beaten back by troops under the leadership of Captain István Dobó. But after five more attacks, the castle finally fell in 1596. In 1702, the fortification was blown apart and the castle site became a stone quarry used to rebuild the city. Restoration work, begun more than half a century ago, continues to this day.

Of the many castles in Hungary, this one may have the most dramatic entryway. A cobblestone street forms a ramp leading up to the castle rampart. You can enjoy a good view of the entire town from the castle walls. Turning inward, you will see the **Dobó István Bastion** and the **Bishop's Palace**. The **Castle Museum** collection inside the palace includes tapestries, copper vessels from the Turkish period, handicrafts, and devices used to torture and execute prisoners. It is open Tuesday through Sunday from 10:00 a.m. to 6:00 p.m. A separate art gallery in a nearby building has excellent landscapes of Transylvania. While it is fun to visit the museum, the castle grounds are the number one attraction here. Among the ruins are the remains of **Sultan Valide's Baths**. Of special interest are guided tours, including some conducted in English, leading through the castle's subterranean passageways. This is one of the great underground tours of Eastern Europe.

West of the castle on Harangonto utca is Eger's famous **minaret**. It marks the northern European boundary of the Ottoman empire. For a closer look and a view of the city, walk inside this 110-foot-high column and climb to the top. To get inside, ask for the key at the front desk at the Minaret Hotel.

One of three Hungarian archbishoprics, Eger is a treasure house of religious art and architecture. While baroque architecture dominates the town, a number of other important styles are in evidence. For example, the baroque architecture of the seventeenth-century **Archepiscopal Palace** at Szabadság tér and Széchenyi utca was complemented with a neoclassical addition in the eighteenth

Cobblestone approach to the Eger Castle, Hungary

century. The Basilica on Szabadság tér, one of the largest churches in Hungary, is another neoclassical landmark. Opposite the cathedral is the late baroque **Lyceum**, a teacher's college built in the eighteenth century. Visit the romantic courtyard and then step inside to see the frescoed ceiling of heaven in the former north wing chapel. Be sure to see the library in the south wing also. The eleven-story observatory tower has a **museum of astronomy**, and, near the top, an observation point equipped with a telescope.

As you explore Eger, you will discover many important treasures. This is also a town full of architectural grace notes, such as the crested eighteenth-century rococo wrought-iron gate at **County Hall** and artful doorways on the **Franciscan Church** and **Rottenstein mansion** on Széchenyi utca. And after sightseeing, relax in the **thermal baths** on the west side of Népkert Park.

Eger is also the gateway to popular Hungarian resort towns. To the northwest is the village of Szarvasko. Continue to Szilvásvárad, a former estate that is popular for its narrow-gauge excursion train. To the north are the Bukk Mountains, cresting at about 2,900 feet.

The baroque Hotel Kastely Szirak, in Szirak, northern Hungary

There is a national park and wildlife refuge here. And you can enjoy caving, boating, excursion trains, skiing, and, in the spring months, beautiful wildflower panoramas. For a big splurge, you can stay at the luxurious **Palota Szálló** at Lillafüred, northeast of Eger near Miskolc. Tel. 46/54433. Set on a small lake, the hotel is surrounded by a terraced hanging garden and park.

Sopron

M any visitors to Western Europe fail to appreciate just how easy it is to sample the pleasures of the East. Just 40 miles south of Vienna, Sopron is an easy day trip for visitors to the Austrian capital. It is also a convenient hub for excursions to Köszeg and the Esterházy Palace at Fertöd. Of course, you can also make the 130-mile (3-hour) journey here from Budapest. No matter which way you come, Sopron is bound to be a highlight of your trip to Europe.

Sopron was settled by the Romans, and it is one of the few major destinations in Hungry that was never taken by the Turks. Unlike Budapest or Eger, it was never sacked, and the historic Old Town remains intact. Although most Americans have never heard of Western Transdanubia or Sopron, it is a well-known holiday spot in Europe. And why not? With over 100 monuments, a car-free Old Town, historic churches, museums, and Roman ruins, Sopron is a delight. It also offers easy access to the picturesque Lövér Mountains. While prices here are far better than in neighboring Austria, you can still expect to travel in comfort.

GETTING THERE

From Vienna there is direct train service from the Sudbanhof via Wiener Neustadt as well as bus service. Express trains also reach Sopron via Györ. If you are driving, allow three hours.

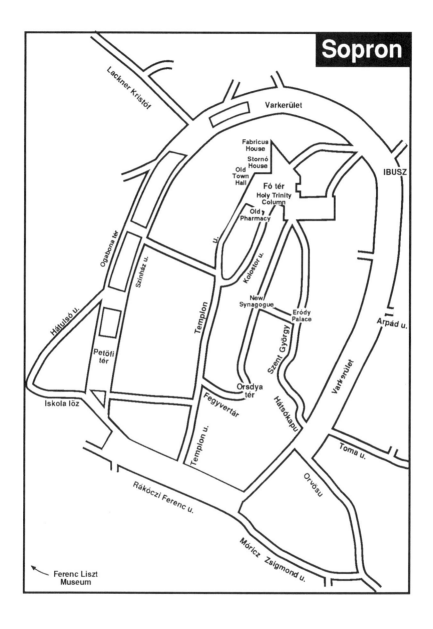

LODGING

Hotel Sopron at #7 Fovenyverem utca runs 5,180 forints ($72). Tel. 99/14254; fax 99/11090. **Hotel Lövér** at #4 Varisi utca charges 4,464 forints ($62). Tel. 99/11061; fax 99/12551. **Hotel Palatinus** at #23 Új utca charges 3,450 forints ($48). Tel. 99/11395. **Hotel Jegverem** at #1 Jeverem utca runs 2,160 forints ($30). Tel. 99/12004. In the budget category is the **Lövér Turistaszálló** on Pócsi domb offering dorm accommodations for 388 forints ($5.40). Tel. 99/11715. Rooms in private homes and apartments can be arranged through **Ibusz** at #41 Varkerulet. Tel. 99/12455. Homestays can also be arranged through **Ciklámen Tourist** at #8 Ógabona tér. Tel. 99/12040. The **Lövér Campground** is about two miles south of the center on Pócsi domb. Tel. 99/11715. Take bus #12 from Jagus 1 tér.

A luxurious alternative in Nagycenk, about seven miles south of Sopron, is the **Kastélyszällö Nagycenk**, a mansion favored by Count Istvan Szechenyi (1791–1860), the reform period intellectual who has been called "the greatest Hungarian." It is blessed with formal gardens and a fountain. Tel. 97–41586.

FOOD

The Taverna is located at #15 Táncsics Mihály utca. Tel. 99/11620. Another good choice is **Rondella étterem**, #12–14 Szent György utca. Tel. 99/12346. Also recommended are **Szélmalom étterem**, #1 Fraknói utca (tel. 99/11023), and **Gamnbrinus étterem** at #3 Fö tér (tel. 99/11697).

SIGHTSEEING

Historic Sopron has enough attractions to keep you busy for days. The only question is where to begin. Why not start at the **Ferenc Liszt Museum** at Május 1 tér. Exhibits include painting, handicrafts, local history, Hungarian archaeology, and ethnography. There is also a small exhibit on the Hungarian composer. Tel. 99/11463. Open Tuesday through Sunday from 10:00 a.m. to 6:00 p.m. April through September and 10:00 a.m. to 5:00 p.m. October through March. Like all museum hours in Sopron, these are subject to change. Be sure to confirm them through the Ibusz office.

Sopron, Hungary

From the Liszt Museum, continue north to **Old Town** (Belvaros). This is the city's star attraction. You can explore narrow streets lined with historic buildings dating to the sixteenth century. A good place for a view is the top of the baroque **Firewatch Tower** which also has an interesting exhibit. The original structure, begun in the twelfth century, was rebuilt following a fire in 1676.

Be sure to explore Fö tér, the heart of Old Town. On or near this square are a wine cellar, a mining museum, and the Gothic **Goat Church**, one of the town's most important landmarks. Goat crests appear in the coat of arms of the family that commissioned construction of this thirteenth-century church. Another Old Town pleasure is visiting some of the famous buildings dating to the fifteenth century. On Fö tér, they include the baroque **Fabricius House** at #6 where you can see Roman sculptures. Tel. 99/11327. The nearby Renaissance palace at #8 is the **Storno House**, which has exhibits on Sopron history as well as fine art collections. Tel. 99/11327. Another notable Fö tér building of more recent vintage is the **City Hall**, where, if you're in luck, you may catch a wedding in progress.

Another major street in Sopron is Szent György utca, home of the onetime **Erdödy Palace**. Located at #16, this rococo landmark is a good photo opportunity. Nearby is the **Gothic Church of St. George**. Continue south to the Orsolya Church and then loop back north to the **New Synagogue** at #22 Új utca. Sopron's Jews were forced out in the early sixteenth century, and this building remained in private hands until the end of World War II. It now serves as a Judaic museum. Tel. 99/11463. Be sure to stroll the northern end of Varkerület, where you'll find some of the city's most notable rococo and baroque commercial buildings and apartments. Among them is the **Golden Eagle Pharmacy** at #29.

Fö tér, Sopron, Hungary

Köszeg

Thirty miles south of Sopron, at the foot of the Alps, is Köszeg, one of the most intriguing small towns in Hungary. The community's greatest moment came in 1532 when a local garrison held off a vast Turkish unit in a David and Goliath battle. The victory was a decisive one that prevented the Ottoman Empire from moving on Vienna. Although Köszeg is smaller than Sopron, its appeal is similar. The city's best-known landmark is the fourteenth-century Jurisch Castle.

GETTING THERE

Direct bus service links Köszeg with Sopron. The trip takes about 90 minutes. There is also train service from Budapest via Szombathely.

LODGING

Hotel Irottkö, at #4 Fö tér, is a modern building with rooms opening onto an atrium lobby. It has the best location in town. Rooms run 3,024 forints ($42). Tel. 94/60373. **Hotel Strucc** at 124 Várköz is a good bet for budget travelers willing to share a bath. Rooms run 1,296 forints ($18). Tel. 94/60323. **Jurisich Turistaház** offers inexpensive dorm accommodations at #9 Rájnis utca. It is open from April 15 to October 15. Tel. 94/60227. For accommodations in private homes or apartments, contact **Savaria Tourist**, at #69 Várköz, tel. 94/60238, or Ibusz, #3 Városház, tel. 94/12455. **Strand Camping** is located at #79 Also krt. Tel. 94/60981.

FOOD

Try **Bécsikapu Sōprōzo** at #5 Rájnis Jozsef for steak, wienerschnitzel, boar, or pizza. You will enjoy patio dining in warm weather. Tel. 94/60297. Other possibilities include the **Park étterem** at #2 Park utca (tel. 94/60367) and the **Gesztenyés étterem** at #23 Rákóczi ferenc utca (tel. 94/60369).

SIGHTSEEING

From Köztarsaság tér, head north through the archway of the **Heroes' Tower**. Built in 1932 on the 400th anniversary of the town's legendary defeat of the Turks, this gate is the entryway to cobbled **Jurisich tér**. The Gothic **Church of St. James** fronts on this square. Be sure to see the fifteenth-century frescoes inside. Also on the square is the **Church of St. Emerich**, a blend of baroque, Gothic, and Renaissance architecture. The **Miklós Jurisics Museum** at #4 re-creates century-old businesses including a print shop, a candy store, and a watch shop. It is open Tuesday through Sunday from 10:00 a.m. to 6:00 p.m. Also of special interest is the Gothic **Town Hall** at #8.

From the square, go north on Chernel utca, past some of Köszeg's finest baroque homes, to the **Castle** at #9 Rájnis József utca. Another blend of baroque, Gothic, and Renaissance, this famous building was reconstructed thirty years ago. It is open Tuesday through Sunday from 10:00 a.m. to 6:00 p.m. It now serves as a museum, a cultural center, and a hostel. The castle's Renaissance **museum** wing is the best place to learn the story of Köszeg's fascinating history. Try to arrange an English-speaking guide through Savaria Tourist (see Lodging, above). It is hard to predict what you might find inside these famous walls surrounded by a dry moat. On the day I stopped by, a children's choir was performing in the auditorium, while down in the courtyard teens listened to the strains of Tina Turner blaring from a Blaupunkt tape deck inside a customized Lada, the Soviet car made in joint venture with Italy.

Before leaving Western Transdanubia, consider two other possibilities. Nagycenk, eight miles southeast of Sopron on route 84, is the home of the **Széchenyi Museum Railroad** commemorating Count István Széchenyi. The man who brought steam railroading to Hungary, the count also helped link Buda and Pest through his successful campaign to build the Chain Bridge in Budapest. The rail museum has a narrow gauge train that runs to Fertöboz. There is a bus link between Sopron and Nagycenk, and you can stay in the **Kastélyszálló Nagycenk**. See Sopron lodging, above.

Finally, no visit to this region is complete without a trip to Fertöd and the **Esterházy Palace**. With 126 rooms in a horseshoe shape, this baroque residence ranks as an Eastern European Versailles. The Esterházys, who married well, loved to entertain. Although the Communists bounced the noble family after World War II, the new regime did clean up the ravages of the Nazis. Today you can see the palace in its original splendor. In addition, court composer Joseph Haydn is memorialized in the palace museum. (Esterházy descendants have made a name for themselves on the Hungarian national soccer team.) From mid-April to mid-October, the castle is open from 8:00 a.m. to noon and 1:00 p.m. to 5:00 p.m. In the off-season, it closes at 4:00 p.m.

Although the Esterházy Palace is fit or a king or queen, you can stay here for a song. It's the least expensive of Hungary's castle and mansion hotels. A dozen modest dorm-style rooms are available for about 720 forints ($10). While there is nothing elegant about these shared bath accommodations, you may appreciate the convenience of staying here. Book well in advance. Tel. 99/45971. Or write to Kastélyszálló #2 Bartók Béla utca, 9431 Fertöd.

Yugoslavia

Long one of the most popular destinations in Eastern Europe, Yugoslavia is famous for its romantic Adriatic coast and splendid mountains, parks, lakes, and waterfalls. Its most famous resorts are only a short distance from off-the-beaten-track villages, monasteries, and parks that will give you a chance to experience the nation's unreconstructed past. Its fascinating political, religious, and architectural history create a compelling backdrop that will add to your understanding and enjoyment of this region. Walking the walled villages and visiting historic districts where cars are not allowed, you will be able to step back in time and get a sense of what Europe was like before the arrival of the freeway, the supermarket, and the jet charter. If you are looking for sun and sea, the Dalmatian Coast has the classic mild Mediterranean climate, and its coastal waters are the cleanest on the entire Adriatic. The coastline stretches all the way from Italy to Albania, over one thousand miles as the crow flies, double that if you allow for its deep bays and coves.

Yugoslavia, a nation of 22.5 million, shares its border with seven countries: Greece, Albania, Italy, Austria, Hungary, Romania, and Bulgaria. Only a unified state since 1918, six autonomous republics compose Yugoslavia: Slovenia, Croatia, Macedonia, Bosnia, Serbia, and Montenegro. Two, Slovenia and Croatia, are in the process of secession.

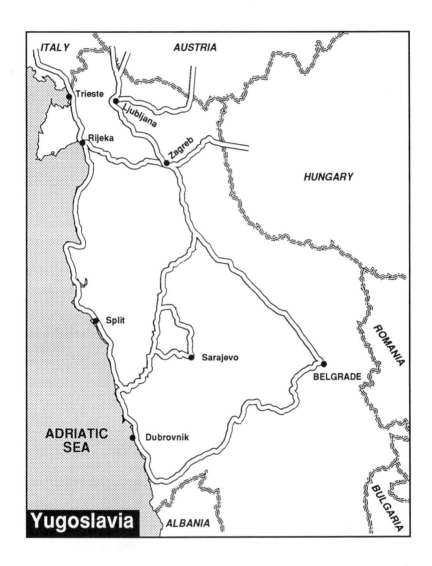

Although Yugoslavia means "South Slav," this nation is a European and Occidental melting pot. Thus, Bosnia and Serbia show the characteristics of the Ottoman Empire and Slovenia the mark of Austro-Hungary, while Istria and Dalmatia bear the influence of Venetian domination in folk culture, architecture, and food. Ethnic rivalry and unrest have led to separatist movements for autonomy by the individual republics. Indeed, the political map of this nation is still being reconfigured as secessionist groups Balkanize this land. As in the Soviet Union, some of the republics are breaking away from the central government and opting for autonomous self-government. These political changes are taking place against a background of high inflation aimed at strengthening the nation's transition to a market economy.

The country's great hero is Marshal Tito, who, after leading the Partisan forces against the Nazis during World War II, presided over the country until his death in 1980. Under his leadership, this non-aligned nation split off from the Soviet-dominated Eastern Bloc and supported a new brand of socialism that resembled Lenin's New Economic Policy. Tito's self-managed socialism also encouraged Western investment, a factor that helped build the nation's tourist infrastructure. Today his picture hangs in homes, offices, and public buildings across the land.

Dubrovnik

The ancient walled city of Dubrovnik is the premier jewel of the spectacular Dalmatian Coast. Rimmed by the chalky Dinaric Alps and the azure waters of the Adriatic, this city has the timeless appeal of Venice, Jerusalem, and Kyoto. The only way to explore Dubrovnik is on foot, a fact of life that adds to the many pleasures of exploring the city's narrow streets, monasteries, cathedrals, and palatial museums. The stone streets, rubbed smooth by footsteps of pedestrians over the centuries, gleam in the morning light. With its waterfront lookouts, fountains, terra-cotta tiles,

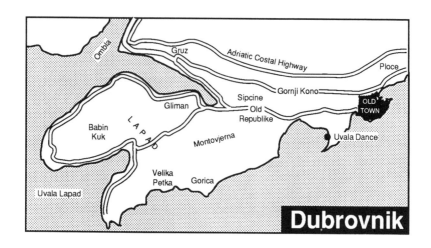

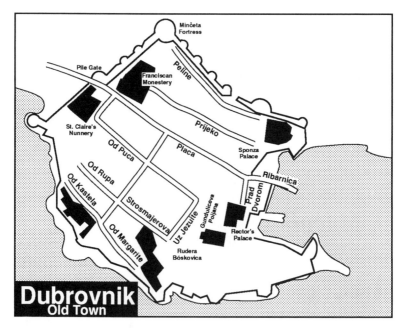

and Renaissance monuments, Dubrovnik is a perfect way to round out a visit to Eastern Europe. Or, if your time is limited, consider adding it on to a visit to Italy, an easy plane, train, or ferry ride away. Dubrovnik is just one hour by air from Rome.

Although Dubrovnik is now best known for its architectural and historic splendor, it was once an Adriatic political hub. Formerly Ragusa, a city-state that rivaled Venice in its reach and influence, it maintained its integrity and semiautonomy by paying tribute to the dominant powers. Founded in the seventh century A.D. by refugees from the Graeco-Roman city of Epidaurus (now Cavtat), it took the name of the island on which it was built (Ragusa) and gradually expanded to the adjacent oak-wooded mainland. In 1180, Ragusa elected a prince and began its consolidation of power, making trade agreements with the nearby Balkan provinces and alliances with the Adriatic pirates for defense against Venice, their powerful enemy, while strengthening its naval and commercial influence in the region. At one point, the ships in its fleet numbered over 2,000.

Ever resourceful, after its conquest by Venice in 1205, the city-state maintained independence by paying tribute to one sovereign state after another—Venice, Hungary, the Ottoman Turks—while continuing to thrive as a maritime republic and prosperous trading power. As it pursued a policy of enlightened, some say Machiavellian, self-interest in its conduct of external affairs, the republic followed a progressive course with its own citizenry. For example, it established a home for the aged and abolished slave trade well ahead of other nearby nations. The republic was governed by a Grand Council, headed by a chief of state called a rector. This rotating post combined the duties of president and magistrate.

In 1667, not long after Ragusa changed its name to Dubrovnik (*Dubrova* means oakwood), an earthquake tumbled the city walls, destroying a major part of the city and its population. The republic survived its enemy advances while it rebuilt, maintaining its independence for another century until Austria ceded most of Dalmatia to Napoleon at the beginning of the nineteenth century. Dubrovnik's leaders did not relinquish control of their city-state quietly. A last minute appeal was submitted to the Congress of Vienna, but the Hapsburgs refused to hear this desperate plea. Control of Dubrovnik and the rest of Dalmatia returned to Austria in 1815. But the city's proud nobility continued to protest the occupation. Many of Dubrovnik's noble families made their feelings known by refusing to marry or have children that could carry on their dynasty. A century later, in 1918, Dubrovnik became part of the modern Yugoslav state.

Now busloads of tourists throng the city in the high season, cruise ships stop here, large modern resort hotels lie to its north and south. Yet the laundry hanging from balcony to balcony across narrow streets, the thriving early morning market, the daily gatherings of youth along the Plaka at dusk all demonstrate that this city is not merely a prettily preserved historical artifact but an urban center rich with vibrant, ongoing life.

HELPFUL HINT

Although the Dubrovnik area has remained safe, secessionist battles elsewhere in Yugoslavia make it a good idea to check with the U.S. State Department in Washington (202-647-5225) before visiting this country. You can obtain the same traveler's advisories from your local passport office or through the computerized reservation service of many travel agencies. This information is also available from American embassies throughout Europe.

ARRIVAL

By Air: JAT, the Yugoslav national airlines, provides service to Dubrovnik from the United States and European cities such as Rome. In addition, many European carriers also provide service to Belgrade and Zagreb where you can connect to Dubrovnik. JAT has an office just outside the Pile Gate.

By Bus: Intercity buses are frequent, inexpensive, and reliable but not luxurious. The Dubrovnik bus terminal (tel. 23-088) is located in Gruž, near the harbor, about a 20-minute bus or taxi ride from Stari Grad. There is also a good network of city buses. All buses charge a supplement for luggage. Excursions by bus to nearby attractions can be arranged through several travel agencies located in or near Old Town.

By Boat: Excursion boats to nearby islands leave frequently from the small harbor just outside the city walls, but the major nautical activity takes place at the harbor at Gruž. From here you can catch the wonderful ferry that travels up and down the coast daily in season, stopping at Korčula, Split, Hvar, Rab, and Rijecka. Jadrolina also has an overnight ferry from Dubrovnik to Greece, stopping at Corfu, Igoumenitsa, and Piraeus (book ahead at high season), and some Greek ships service this route as well. Connections can also be made from Gruž to Venice. In addition, a number of ferries connect Yugoslavian ports with the Italian Adriatic ports of Bari, Pescara, and Ancona. International Cruise Center in Mineola, New York, has information on Yugoslav ship and ferry service. Tel. (516) 747-8880. Or contact the Yugoslav National Tourist Office at 630 Fifth Avenue, New York, NY 10111. Tel. (212) 757-2801.

The Dalmatian Coast, with its many offshore islands, hidden coves, and pretty harbors, is a sailor's paradise. For boat rental, inquire at the Marina Dubrovnik, Komolac bb, 50236 Dubrovnik, Mokosica. Tel. 50/87-722. Navigational charts and the *Navigational Guide to the Adriatic* ($6 and very useful) are available at the marine bookstore.

By Rail: There are no trains into Dubrovnik. The nearest major railroad station is at Kardeljevo, 110 kilometers up the coast. There are frequent bus connections from Dubrovnik to Kardeljevo, where you can make train connections to inland cities. For information and ticket sales, call Atlas, Pile 1 (tel. 27-333), or consult the Yugoslav National Tourist Office.

Dubrovnik, Yugoslavia

By Car: Because of the secessionist politics playing out in the country these days, we suggest that you travel to Dubrovnik via plane or ship and then rent a car locally. A good way to get here from Italy is to take one of the car ferries available from Adriatic ports like Bari. Cars can be rented at the Dubrovnik airport through Kompas-Hertz (tel. 77-284) and other companies. Foreign tourists can buy gas at a discount with coupons obtainable at the border. Cars are not permitted in Old Town, which is the city core, but there are several all-day parking lots outside the city walls.

Here is a partial list of unleaded gas stations. You can obtain a complete list at border points or from any ADAC auto club office in Germany. Make it a point never to drive with less than half a tank. Always try to buy gas before 6:00 p.m.

City	Station
Belgrade	Ibarska magist. Zar
	Lipovacka suma, Bgd.-Lazarevac
Crikvenica	Umfahrung
Dubrovnik-Dubad	Put Vladim. Nazora
Gvegelija	Gevgleija
Kozina	Krvavi potok 1
Ljubljana	Hraska Str. 13
	Barje I
Novi Sad	Maksima Gorkog
Novska	Motorway
Ohrid	Podmolje
Postojna	Motorway
Rijeka	Kantrida II
Sarajevo	Hrasno
Sentilj	Sentilj 56
Skopje	Partizanski odreda bb
Split	Ul. Prvoboraca
Subotica	Aleksandrovo
Titograd	Titograd II
Zadar	Murvica-Magistrate
Zagreb	Ljubljanska aveniga
	Trg. Marka Oreskovica

MONEY

The dinar is the Yugoslav currency. One U.S. dollar is worth 10 dinars. Even though inflation is high, exchange rates are adjusted accordingly, so the trick is never to buy more dinars than you will need immediately. There are bargains to be had in this country, especially off-season, when hotel rooms and full or half pension arrangements are often available at half the high-season rate.

Tipping is customary in restaurants. We recommend that in addition to dinars you carry some cash in small denomination dollars or German marks.

GENERAL INFORMATION

You will find the Yugoslav National Tourist office in the corner building to your right as you enter the Pile Gate. Tel. 050/26-302. Here you can buy maps, change money, find out about rooms in private homes, and buy inexpensive concert tickets, books, and postcards. When you request information about transportation and other matters, the quality and mood of the response varies considerably with the personnel! As a general rule, information you do not specifically ask for will not be volunteered, even if it seems obvious that it might be of use to you. So ask, ask, and ask, and if you do not get satisfaction, come back later when someone else is behind the desk.

Atlas, Pile 1 (tel. 27-333); **Kompas**, Marsala Tita 14 (tel. 23-186); and **Yugotours**, Lucarica 1 (tel. 24-966) all handle excursions and other bookings.

GETTING AROUND

There are six taxi stands conveniently located in the city. Taxis operate on a meter, with the rates higher at night. If you call a taxi, the meter starts running at the taxi station. It is always a good policy to get a price estimate from the driver before you begin your trip.

TELEPHONE

As with all calls from the United States, you must first dial 011 followed by the country code (38), the city code (50), and the number. Thus, a call to 654/386 would be made by dialing 011-38-50-654/386. Remember, for long distance calls within the country, you must dial a 0 before the city code. Long distance phone service is spotty. Try to call during off-peak hours.

LODGING

Hotel accommodations can be expensive in Dubrovnik during peak season. Off-season, they may drop as much as 35 percent. In the Ploce district, the **Argentina** is situated right on the water. Tel. 50/23-855, fax 50/32-524. Expect to spend $150. In the same area is the **Villa Dubrovnik** (tel. 50/22-933, fax 50/32-524). Rooms run about $125. Near the Pile Gate is the elegant old **Grand Hotel Imperial** (tel. 50/28-655, fax 50/28-655), ideally located but with nightly loud music on the terrace. Rooms run about $75. In the same price range is the **Dubravka** (tel. 50/26-293, fax 50/26-284), the only hotel within the walls of Old Town. Many more modern hotels are situated along the coast and in nearby Cavtat. A complete listing can be obtained from the Yugoslav National Tourist Office, 630 Fifth Avenue, New York, NY 10111, tel. 212/757-2802. At many of the hotels, a full board or half-board arrangement is available.

Accommodations can also be obtained in private homes. These often provide a more personalized glimpse into the life of the country. The YTO offices, on the Plaka near the Pile Gate, will provide names and addresses, but at the bus stop at the Pile Gate or the bus station at Gruz, apartment owners often come personally to seek out their clientele. Prices will usually be quoted in deutsche marks, and marks or dollars are happily accepted. It is of course quite all right, even advisable, to ask to see the room before you agree to rent it. Rates generally run $25 to $35. During the high season, there is usually a 30 percent surcharge for any stay less than three days. We believe these private homestays are a best buy for midrange travelers.

The city also has a campground, Auto-Camp "Solitudo." Tel 50/22-666.

FOOD

There are many restaurants that cater to tourists in the Stari Grad. In fact, it is hard to find one that does not. The busiest restaurant street is Prijeko, which runs parallel to the Plaka and is lined colorfully with outdoor tables, wall to wall. Here prices and menus are remarkably similar, although annoying touts will try to convince you that you should go no farther than their establishment. More low key—and less expensive—are the outdoor restaurants located in the square by Orlando's statue. The outdoor cafés that line the

Plaka are a great place to people watch. Don't neglect to explore the pleasant restaurants outside the walls of Stari Grad. Dubrovnik is not a gourmet paradise, but the quality of the food is generally high. Fish is sold by weight in restaurants and is generally expensive. Calamari and scampi are more plentiful and cheaper. The generic southern European tourist menu of pork cutlet, spaghetti bolognese, pizza, and so on, is much in evidence. Among the local specialties are *cevapcici* (small, spicy, grilled meatballs), *raznjici* (grilled pork or veal kebabs), and a squid ink risotto. The dessert specialty in restaurants is a crêpe called *palačinke*. There is an excellent ice cream shop near Onofrio's fountain, the *International Herald Tribune* is sold nearby, and various bakeries running to puff pastries and whipping cream can be found. Coffee is a choice between the strong, gritty Turkish stuff served in thimbles, Nescafé, or ersatz cappuccino. Name your poison. Tea is not a beverage much understood in this country.

Yugoslavia produces excellent wine, both red and white. For a red, try Peljesac. A pleasant white is Grk, made on Korčula, which has a faint flavor of woodruff. Mineral water and soft drinks are available, and the tap water is fine.

For picnics, make a leisurely trip through the morning market to buy fruit and cheese (sold by the kilo or half kilo, not the piece). Pick up whatever else you need—bread, chocolate, yogurt, paper goods—in the small "supermarkets."

For steaks, try **Domino's**, an expensive restaurant inside the walled city at #3 Domino. Tel. 50/32-832. In the same price range is **Nautika**, a seafood restaurant on Pile Street near the gate. For Dalmatian fare, try **Prijeko**, a moderate restaurant on Prijeko Street in the old city. Also on Prijeko Street is **Wanda**, a restaurant serving Dalmatian and continental food.

NIGHTLIFE

The **Dubrovnik Summer Festival**, which takes place from mid-July to late August, offers over one hundred plays, concerts, and folk dance performances. Concerts are also frequently scheduled at other times of the year. Reasonably priced tickets can be booked through the tourist office. In September and October, **Musical Autumn** concerts are performed in the Rector's Palace, a splendid location.

Call the Yuvoslav National Tourist office in New York for details. Most of the major nightclubs are found in hotels like the **Libertas** at Ulica I.L. Lavcevicka i. Tel. 50/27-444. Here you will find the **Tarantela** nightclub and the **Ragusina** taverna.

SIGHTSEEING

Dubrovnik does not overwhelm the visitor with museums and monuments. Its appeal lies in its elegant proportions, its suddenly changing light, the discovery of an exquisite bit of stone statuary niched into a wall or fountain, the ever-changing stage of café life. All this you will discover as you make your way inside the wall of Stari Grad, or Old Town.

The main entrance to Old Town is the Pile Gate, on the west side of Stari Grad. The Pile is approached by a handsome stone bridge spanning a moat (no cars are allowed inside the city walls). The broad stone seats that line the bridge make it a convenient place to meet someone or people watch. Street vendors often congregate at the entrance to the city peddling whistles and balloons.

The main street of Stari Grad, the Plaka, is one of the loveliest small-scale human thoroughfares in the world. It extends from the Pile Gate to the clock tower. The beautiful facades flanking this walkway house elegant shops selling leather and embroidered goods and sidewalk cafés. Tourists and shoppers continue the work of centuries, polishing and wearing down the marble street to a burnished luminescence. In the early evening the sightseers are replaced by the youth of the city, hanging out, smoking, looking each other over, like their counterparts anywhere.

The wall has major entrances on opposite sides of the city, the Pile Gate and the Ploče Gate. Begin at the stairway to the left of the Pile Gate, where you can buy a ticket for a few dinars. The gate itself is an imposing complex of arches and stairways. We recommend that you go as early as possible (the wall is open at 10:00 a.m.), since it becomes hot and crowded during the peak tourist season. As it is under constant repair, you may see work crews chiseling away at new stone blocks to give them a historic look. On our visit we saw a dozen blue-jacketed young stonemasons seated at noon at a makeshift table around a caldron of soup. A couple of their mates sprawled face down nearby for a nap in the sun, oblivious to the

Rector's Palace, Dubrovnik, Yugoslavia

Dubrovnik, Yugoslavia

gawking tourists above. Be sure to take your camera to the top where you can look down on beautiful red tiled roofs, church spires, the citys narrow streets, and the Adriatic coast.

To your right as you enter the Pile Gate is the fifteenth-century **Onofrio Fountain**, a popular meeting place that looks like a small mosque. To the left is the **Franciscan Monastery**, famous for its treasury painting that shows a good view of the city prior to the 1667 earthquake that demolished much of the town. The monastery's delicately arched and columned Romanesque cloister is particularly beautiful. The monks were required to have a pharmacy on the premises. **Franjevacka Apotkeka**, Yugoslavia's oldest apothecary and the third oldest in Europe, operates still. The varnished cases are inlaid with beautiful designs, and on the shelves are hand-painted apothecary jars. Of the many pharmacy museums in Europe, this one may be the most impressive. Try to see one of the concerts performed in the monastery church. Tickets can be obtained at the tourist office or at the door.

Stroll down the Plaka, browsing in shops that sell elegant leather goods, crystal, and embroidery work. Handsome books on Yugoslav art are a particular bargain, and mailing can be arranged in the shops. Sidewalk cafés are numerous here, and they are the best places to people watch, especially in the early evening when the city residents follow the Mediterranean tradition of a slow stroll through the streets. (Long live populations that are not locked into their homes by television!) The people of Dubrovnik are particularly handsome. The clothes and carriage of the women echo their elegant Italian neighbors across the water, and men have a proud bearing and vigor that is very appealing. Long used to maintaining their dignity through invasions of foreign visitors, the people we encountered were, for the most part, cordial without being overly friendly.

At the other end of the Plaka you will see the clock tower, with its bronze knights that strike the hour. On the left as you face the clock tower is the **Sponza**, an elegant state building that was first used as a customs house and subsequently as a mint and an academy. Behind the Sponza, near the Ploče Gate, is the **Dominican Monastery**, with its lovely cloisters. Opposite the Sponza is the baroque church of **Sv. Vlaho** (St. Blaise, the patron saint of the city) and, directly across from it, the **City Hall**, which also houses a movie theater, and the immense **Gradska Kafana** (city café). For a pleasant respite, walk through the restaurant to the agreeable terrace overlooking the boat harbor. They serve up a good, if pricey, strudel and an excellent view.

Next to this building is the **Rector's Palace**, with its glorious Renaissance archways and columns. Like many buildings in Dubrovnik, the Rector's Palace has been rebuilt several times following major earthquakes. The result? A happy blending of styles from different periods, in this case, a Renaissance portico attached to a Gothic building. The old republic of Ragusa was governed by a council of 45 merchants, all heads of households over age 50. The rector, chosen from this group, was expected to leave his household and inhabit the palace during the period of his rule. It is a measure of the singularity of purpose expected from him that his rococo bedchamber has only a single bed. The palace also houses displays on the city's maritime and political history as well as a stamp collection and an exhibit of paintings by the city's artists. Concerts are held in the intimate atrium. In the Rector's Palace, time has stopped at 5:45 a.m., marking the moment on May 26, 1808, when the French army occupied the city and put an end to Ragusa's independence.

The Rector's Palace faces onto a narrow sloping square. At the top of the square is the baroque **Cathedral of Our Lady**, whose bells resound against the stone on Sunday morning, scattering the pigeons who flock to the lovely square. The cathedral contains several interesting paintings and relics.

The several streets running parallel to the Plaka on the south side are a shopper's paradise, especially if you like jewelry and fine embroidered goods. Small shops that sell gold, silver filigree, and semiprecious stones abound (the silver is often sold by weight), and bargains can be had in Macedonian rugs and purses made from remnants of old Balkan costumes. Behind the Dubravka Hotel is **Gundulic Poljana**, the square where the old vegetable market is located, worth a trip to see what is available and pick up fresh fruit for your picnic lunch or snack. Here **Orlando's Column**, bearing the figure of a medieval knight in armor, was erected in 1428 as a monument to freedom at a time when the Dubrovnik Republic was besieged by its enemies. Local youth often lounge at its base, as they probably have for centuries.

Other museums within the city walls include the **Ethno-graphic Museum**, which has an outstanding display of folk costumes, and the **Maritime Museum**, where you will find paintings of the city's seafaring tradition. Near the **Serbian Orthodox Church** is the small **Museum of Old Icons**, which brings together icons of the Greek Russian, Venetian, Byzantine, and Boko-Kotor schools.

Outside the city walls you may also want to take the **Atlas Cable Car** up the mountain for a panoramic view of the city.

Excursions from Dubrovnik

Many of the offshore islands of the Dalmatian Coast are easily accessible from Dubrovnik. Day excursions run from the boat harbor in Stari Grad to the nearby Elefite islands: **Sipan, Lopud,** and **Kolocep.** From the main, industrial harbor at Gruz (book ahead at the YTO during high season), you can get a ferry up the coast that stops at **Korčula**, with its exquisite Venetian town that was the birthplace of Marco Polo. This takes about four hours. Or you can go by car or bus to the Trstenik peninsula, for a shorter boat ride. You might consider spending one or two nights on **Korčula**. In addition to the splendid town, you can explore several pleasant fishing villages. The majestic, slightly rundown **Korčula Hotel** (tel. 50/711-078, fax 50/711-746), with its broad veranda, is straight out of a Somerset Maugham novel. It is located right on the water just outside the wall of the Stari Grad (Old Town). At the other end of the harbor are several modern hotels including the **Park** (tel. 50/711-004, fax 50/711-746). For a more remote, tranquil spot, take a bus to Vela Luka (Old Port) and catch the ferry to the verdant island of Lastovo. This island was only recently opened to international tourists because of its military base. There are accommodations at **Hotel Solitudo** (tel. 50/80-002), but we prefer renting a room in an islander's home. Many are located along the coast, with views of the water, reasonable prices, and great hospitality.

Our favorite nearby island is **Mljet**. One end is a national park encompassing two saltwater "lakes." The surrounding white rocks and Aleppo pines make you feel like you are in the Sierras until you swim in the buoyant, tropically warm water. There are day excursions to Mljet from the boat harbor at Dubrovnik. If you decide to stay overnight, accommodations can be arranged at the **Melita**, a monastery that now serves as a hotel. It is located on a tiny island in the lake. Tel. 50/754-315, fax 50/32742. Alternatively, try the modern hotel, **Odisej** (tel. 50/754-205), or a private home.

There are also many excellent mainland excursions from Dubrovnik. Go south down the coastal highway to the spectacular **Bay of Kotor** or inland to the Montenegran capital of **Sarajevo**, rich with Near Eastern mosques and markets. Another possibility is **Mostar**, with its famous Turkish bridge. A few hours north along the coast brings you to the ancient city of **Split**, which has remains of the Diocletian Palace and a vast open market. If you continue up the coast, do not miss the beautiful cathedral at **Sibenik** or the tiny, monument-packed island/peninsula of **Trogir**. All of these are accessible by car or intercity bus if you are an independent traveler. Excursions can be booked through the various tourist offices.

Index

224 / Index

Other Books from John Muir Publications

Adventure Vacations: From Trekking in New Guinea to Swimming in Siberia, Bangs 256 pp. $17.95

Asia Through the Back Door, 3rd ed., Steves and Gottberg 326 pp. $15.95

Belize: A Natural Destination, Mahler, Wotkyns, Schafer 304 pp. $16.95

Buddhist America: Centers, Retreats, Practices, Morreale 400 pp. $12.95

Bus Touring: Charter Vacations, U.S.A., Warren with Bloch 168 pp. $9.95

California Public Gardens: A Visitor's Guide, Sigg 304 pp. $16.95

Catholic America: Self-Renewal Centers and Retreats, Christian-Meyer 325 pp. $13.95

Costa Rica: A Natural Destination, Sheck 280 pp. $15.95 **(2nd ed.** available 3/92 $16.95)

Elderhostels: The Students' Choice, 2nd ed., Hyman 312 pp. $15.95

Environmental Vacations: Volunteer Projects to Save the Planet, Ocko 240 pp. $15.95 **(2nd ed.** available 2/92 $16.95)

Europe 101: History & Art for the Traveler, 4th ed., Steves and Openshaw 372 pp. $15.95

Europe Through the Back Door, 9th ed., Steves 432 pp. $16.95 **(10th ed.** available 1/92 $16.95)

Floating Vacations: River, Lake, and Ocean Adventures, White 256 pp. $17.95

Great Cities of Eastern Europe, Rapoport 240 pp. $16.95

Gypsying After 40: A Guide to Adventure and Self-Discovery, Harris 264 pp. $14.95

The Heart of Jerusalem, Nellhaus 336 pp. $12.95

Indian America: A Traveler's Companion, 2nd ed., Eagle/Walking Turtle 448 pp. $17.95

Mona Winks: Self-Guided Tours of Europe's Top Museums, Steves and Openshaw 456 pp. $14.95

Opera! The Guide to Western Europe's Great Houses, Zietz 296 pp. $18.95

Paintbrushes and Pistols: How the Taos Artists Sold the West, Taggett and Schwarz 280 pp. $17.95

The People's Guide to Mexico, 8th ed., Franz 608 pp. $17.95

The People's Guide to RV Camping in Mexico, Franz with Rogers 320 pp. $13.95

Ranch Vacations: The Complete Guide to Guest and Resort, Fly-Fishing, and Cross-Country Skiing Ranches, 2nd ed., Kilgore 396 pp. $18.95

The Shopper's Guide to Art and Crafts in the Hawaiian Islands, Schuchter 272 pp. $13.95

The Shopper's Guide to Mexico, Rogers and Rosa 224 pp. $9.95

Ski Tech's Guide to Equipment, Skiwear, and Accessories, ed. Tanler 144 pp. $11.95

Ski Tech's Guide to Maintenance and Repair, ed. Tanler 160 pp. $11.95

A Traveler's Guide to Asian Culture, Chambers 224 pp. $13.95

Traveler's Guide to Healing Centers and Retreats in North America, Rudee and Blease 240 pp. $11.95

Understanding Europeans, Miller 272 pp. $14.95

Undiscovered Islands of the Caribbean, 2nd ed., Willes 232 pp. $14.95

Undiscovered Islands of the Mediterranean, Moyer and Willes 232 pp. $14.95

Undiscovered Islands of the U.S. and Canadian West Coast, Moyer and Willes 208 pp. $12.95

A Viewer's Guide to Art: A Glossary of Gods, People, and Creatures, Shaw and Warren 144 pp. $10.95

2 to 22 Days Series
Each title offers 22 flexible daily itineraries that can be used to get the most out of vacations of any length. Included are not only "must see" attractions but also little-known villages and hidden "jewels" as well as valuable general information.

22 Days Around the World, 1992 ed., Rapoport and Willes 256 pp. $12.95
2 to 22 Days Around the Great Lakes, 1992 ed., Schuchter 192 pp. $9.95
22 Days in Alaska, Lanier 128 pp. $7.95
2 to 22 Days in the American Southwest, 1992 ed., Harris 176 pp. $9.95
2 to 22 Days in Asia, 1992 ed., Rapoport and Willes 176 pp. $9.95
2 to 22 Days in Australia, 1992 ed., Gottberg 192 pp. $9.95
22 Days in California, 2nd ed., Rapoport 176 pp. $9.95
22 Days in China, Duke and Victor 144 pp. $7.95
2 to 22 Days in Europe, 1992 ed., Steves 276 pp. $12.95
2 to 22 Days in Florida, 1992 ed., Harris 192 pp. $9.95
2 to 22 Days in France, 1992 ed., Steves 192 pp. $9.95
2 to 22 Days in Germany, Austria, & Switzerland, 1992 ed., Steves 224 pp. $9.95
2 to 22 Days in Great Britain, 1992 ed., Steves 192 pp. $9.95
2 to 22 Days in Hawaii, 1992 ed., Schuchter 176 pp. $9.95
22 Days in India, Mathur 136 pp. $7.95
22 Days in Japan, Old 136 pp. $7.95
22 Days in Mexico, 2nd ed., Rogers and Rosa 128 pp. $7.95
2 to 22 Days in New England, 1992 ed., Wright 192 pp. $9.95
2 to 22 Days in New Zealand, 1991 ed., Schuchter 176 pp. $9.95
2 to 22 Days in Norway, Sweden, & Denmark, 1992 ed., Steves 192 pp. $9.95
2 to 22 Days in the Pacific Northwest, 1992 ed. Harris 192 pp. $9.95
2 to 22 Days in the Rockies, 1992 ed. Rapoport 192 pp. $9.95
2 to 22 Days in Spain & Portugal, 1992 ed., Steves 192 pp. $9.95
22 Days in Texas, Harris 176 pp. $9.95

22 Days in Thailand, Richardson 176 pp. $9.95
22 Days in the West Indies, Morreale and Morreale 136 pp. $7.95

Parenting Series

Being a Father: Family, Work, and Self, *Mothering* Magazine 176 pp. $12.95

Preconception: A Woman's Guide to Preparing for Pregnancy and Parenthood, Aikey-Keller 232 pp. $14.95

Schooling at Home: Parents, Kids, and Learning, *Mothering* Magazine 264 pp. $14.95

Teens: A Fresh Look, *Mothering* Magazine 240 pp. $14.95

"Kidding Around" Travel Guides for Young Readers
Written for kids eight years of age and older.

Kidding Around Atlanta, Pedersen 64 pp. $9.95
Kidding Around Boston, Byers 64 pp. $9.95
Kidding Around Chicago, Davis 64 pp. $9.95
Kidding Around the Hawaiian Islands, Lovett 64 pp. $9.95
Kidding Around London, Lovett 64 pp. $9.95
Kidding Around Los Angeles, Cash 64 pp. $9.95
Kidding Around the National Parks of the Southwest, Lovett 108 pp. $12.95
Kidding Around New York City, Lovett 64 pp. $9.95
Kidding Around Paris, Clay 64 pp. $9.95
Kidding Around Philadelphia, Clay 64 pp. $9.95
Kidding Around San Diego, Luhrs 64 pp. $9.95
Kidding Around San Francisco, Zibart 64 pp. $9.95
Kidding Around Santa Fe, York 64 pp. $9.95
Kidding Around Seattle, Steves 64 pp. $9.95
Kidding Around Spain, Biggs 108 pp. $12.95
Kidding Around Washington, D.C., Pedersen 64 pp. $9.95

Environmental Books for Young Readers
Written for kids eight years of age and older.

The Indian Way: Learning to Communicate with Mother Earth, McLain 114 pp. $9.95

The Kids' Environment Book: What's Awry and Why, Pedersen 192 pp. $13.95

Rads, Ergs, and Cheeseburgers: The Kids' Guide to Energy and the Environment, Yanda 108 pp. $12.95

"Extremely Weird" Series for Young Readers
Written for kids eight years of age and older.

Extremely Weird Bats, Lovett 48 pp. $9.95
Extremely Weird Frogs, Lovett 48 pp. $9.95
Extremely Weird Primates, Lovett 48 pp. $9.95
Extremely Weird Reptiles, Lovett 48 pp. $9.95
Extremely Weird Spiders, Lovett 48 pp. $9.95

Quill Hedgehog Adventures Series
Written for kids eight years of age and older. Our new series of green fiction for kids follows the adventures of Quill Hedgehog and his Animalfolk friends.

Quill's Adventures in the Great Beyond, Waddington-Feather 96 pp. $5.95
Quill's Adventures in Wasteland, Waddington-Feather 132 pp. $5.95
Quill's Adventures in Grozzieland, Waddington-Feather 132 pp. $5.95

Other Young Readers Titles

Kids Explore America's Hispanic Heritage, edited by Cozzens 112 pp. $7.95 (avail. 2/92)

Automotive Repair Manuals

How to Keep Your VW Alive, 14th ed., 440 pp. $21.95
How to Keep Your Subaru Alive 480 pp. $21.95
How to Keep Your Toyota Pickup Alive 392 pp. $21.95
How to Keep Your Datsun/Nissan Alive 544 pp. $21.95

Other Automotive Books

The Greaseless Guide to Car Care Confidence: Take the Terror Out of Talking to Your Mechanic, Jackson 224 pp. $14.95

Off-Road Emergency Repair & Survival, Ristow 160 pp. $9.95

Ordering Information
If you cannot find our books in your local bookstore, you can order directly from us. Please check the "Available" date above. If you send us money for a book not yet available, we will hold your money until we can ship you the book. Your books will be sent to you via UPS (for U.S. destinations). UPS will not deliver to a P.O. Box; please give us a street address. Include $3.25 for the first item ordered and $.50 for each additional item to cover shipping and handling costs. For airmail within the U.S., enclose $4.00. All foreign orders will be shipped surface rate; please enclose $3.00 for the first item and $1.00 for each additional item. Please inquire about foreign airmail rates.

Method of Payment
Your order may be paid by check, money order, or credit card. We cannot be responsible for cash sent through the mail. All payments must be made in U.S. dollars drawn on a U.S. bank. Canadian postal money orders in U.S. dollars are acceptable. For VISA, MasterCard, or American Express orders, include your card number, expiration date, and your signature, or call (800) 888-7504. Books ordered on American Express cards can be shipped only to the billing address of the cardholder. Sorry, no C.O.D.'s. Residents of sunny New Mexico, add 5.875% tax to the total.

Address all orders and inquiries to:
John Muir Publications
P.O. Box 613
Santa Fe, NM 87504
(505) 982-4078
(800) 888-7504